"Jessica Powers' poetry probes the mystery of the human psyche. Her extraordinary poem 'There is a Homelessness' goes to the heart of that indefinable yearning which leads us back to God. How should we read a poem? 'Trust your body!' says Morneau. 'Your body doesn't lie.' Bishop Morneau's fine study explores Powers' sensuous spirituality and helps us to understand how it is that 'poems keep us from capsizing in the storms of life.'"

Dorothy Judd Hall, author
Boston University

"The imagery of Jessica Powers embodies in itself a fascinating introduction to the breathtaking beauty of God's creation and the wonder of divine grace everywhere. Bishop Morneau's guided tour of her world opens the door to some very engaging and often startling transpositions of imagery for the deepest realities of our lives. To pass through these poetic portals is prayer indeed. I heartily recommend the journey!"

Richard J. Sklba
Auxiliary Bishop of Milwaukee

Poetry as Prayer
Jessica Powers

Poetry as Prayer
Jessica Powers

———

by Robert F. Morneau

———

Artwork by Joseph Karlik

Pauline
BOOKS & MEDIA
BOSTON

Library of Congress Cataloging-in-Publication Data

Morneau, Robert F., 1938–
  Poetry as prayer: Jessica Powers / Robert F. Morneau ;
 artwork by Joseph Karlik.
     p.cm. — (The poetry as prayer series)
  Includes bibliographical references.
  ISBN 0-8198-5921-4
   1. Prayers 2. Powers, Jessica. 3. Christian poetry, American.
  I. Title. II. Series.
  BX2182.2 .M6687 2000
  811'.54—dc21

                                                    00-022028

Jessica Powers' poetry and the photo on page 25 are taken
from *The Selected Poetry of Jessica Powers*, published by ICS
Publications, Washington, DC. All copyrights, Carmelite
Monastery, Pewaukee, WI. Used with permission.

Printed and published in the U.S.A. by Pauline Books & Media,
50 Saint Pauls Avenue, Boston, MA 02130-3491.

www.pauline.org

Pauline Books & Media is the publishing house of the Daughters
of St. Paul, an international congregation of women religious
serving the Church with the communications media.

1 2 3 4 5 6   05 04 03 02 01 00

Contents

Foreword

"The Word became flesh and made his dwelling among us…"

Thus Saint John the Evangelist recounts God's definitive entrance into human history in the person of Jesus, the Christ. And to our wonder, the Word still dwells among us, often hidden, sometimes palpably present, expressed in rich and varied forms. Pre-eminent among these forms is the human word: the symbols, speech, utterances, songs that strain to express the ultimate nature of the Word. A somewhat daunting task, for "The Word was in God's presence, and the Word was God." That's where poetry comes in, for according to theologian Rosemary Haughton, poetry is the most accurate way to communicate the incommunicable.

Robert Morneau—bishop, skilled spiritual director, writer, gifted preacher and teacher, lover of books and patron of poetry—has devoted much of his life to creating a communion between the Word dwelling within, and "outer words," between the life of prayer and the stunning truth of poetry. He himself embodies these two realities. When he writes that, "symbols, images, metaphors, analogies change our lives," he does so with conviction, for he knows that poetry can usher us into the Divine Presence. Poetry *can* be prayer.

Bishop Morneau has chosen to illustrate this truth through the life and work of the Carmelite poet Jessica Powers. It was he who introduced me to her poetry fifteen years ago, an introduction that led me to probe more deeply into the life-story and longings of a woman who fashioned exquisite lyrics in the silence and solitude of a religious cloister. For that introduction, I am forever grateful. Now readers will be grateful to him for the new and penetrating light he sheds on many of Jessica Powers' poems and their relation to the context of her vowed religious life.

In this new book on *Poetry as Prayer*, the author uncovers the deep interiority of Powers' lyrics. Clearly, her poems (she calls them "songs") grew out of her own experiences, and in them the twists and turns of her life journey are evident. It can be honestly said that she wrote her life in rhythm and rhyme. What Morneau does, however, is to name the movements of soul that pressed this nun-poet into the world of words. The inner stirrings of humility and joyousness, of compassion and forgiveness, of vastness and infinity…these he names as signs of God with her—and with us. He shows how concentration on the particular—a bird, a tree, a transient feeling—moved Jessica toward the universal, toward nothing less than God.

Morneau recognizes that Jessica Powers' inner world was not like a walled-off garden, demanding utter privacy. In so doing, he renders a great service to contemplatives who often are mistakenly thought to be "out of it." His probing of the substance of Powers' solitude reveals her authentic sensitivity for those on the margins.

An illustration is the poem "There Is a Homelessness," which deals with the true roots of homelessness. "It is more than having no place of one's own, no bed or chair. / It is more than walking in a waste of wind, / or gleaning the crumbs where someone else has dined." Anyone who has spent time in a homeless shelter knows the truth of those lines. The homeless who seek haven and food (and who deserve to receive these necessities) need so much more. They, like all of us, experience homelessness in what Jessica Powers termed "the loneliness of mystery." One is reminded of the words of the late Dom Helda

Camera: the poor deserve more than the crumbs from our tables. They, like us who live amidst plenty, also desire relationships, and at the deepest level, desire to be at peace in God's presence.

Fans of Jessica Powers will find new depths in these pages. first time readers will benefit from the finest of introductions to her work. And something more awaits *all* readers. Being an experienced teacher and spiritual guide, the author knows that many will need some help in approaching poetry as prayer. A whole chapter, therefore, is devoted to suggestions for this new way of praying. One suggestion is to memorize poems or portions thereof. "When something is put to memory," Morneau writes, "an intimacy begins to grow that can be truly transformative." I know that to be true of the author. I have been present when his preaching or lecturing moved effortlessly into poetry especially suited to the moment. Briefly, fleetingly, he *was* the poem—and so were the listeners.

While Jessica Powers' poetry is the focus of this fine book, Bishop Morneau also includes a list of other poets whose poems have inspired him. One poet, Mary Oliver, is also a favorite of mine. Oliver believes a poem must have sincere energy and a spiritual purpose, and she wants poems to ask questions that the reader will feel compelled to answer. She could speak for Jessica Powers, and indeed, for Robert Morneau who, with this new book, invites the reader into reflection and dialogue—an invitation well worth accepting.

Dolores R. Leckey Senior Fellow,
Woodstock Theological Center,
Georgetown University

(Author of *Winter Music: A Life of Jessica Powers*)

Introduction

On January 26, 1999, Pope John Paul II addressed 22,000 young people in Kiel Arena, St. Louis: "You belong to Christ and he has called you by name. Your first responsibility is to get to know as much as you can about him. You get to know him truly and personally only through prayer. What is needed is that you talk to him, and listen to him."

A shiver went down my spine as I watched the youth of our nation respond to this challenge. Prayer is about our relationship with God; prayer is "simply" entering into dialogue—speaking and listening; prayer is a door through which we must go to encounter deeply the mystery of our triune God.

Eight weeks after this event in St. Louis, John Paul II wrote a letter to the artists of the world. He expressed his esteem for their vocation and prayed that a fruitful dialogue between faith and art might enrich our world. One field of art is poetry. Down through the ages, poets have played a significant role in expressing their faith in verse. We are the beneficiaries.

Prayer, the dialogue between God and humankind, has many sources. God speaks and elicits a response through the mystery of creation. Many individuals find nature—the beauty of a sunrise or sunset, the arch of a rainbow, the vastness of the ocean, the lure of the desert, a simple blade of grass—a stimulus for prayer. Wonder, awe, and reverence flood the heart as we stroll through the marvels of creation.

Others turn to Sacred Scripture as the primary well-spring for hearing God's voice and feeling God's call. In pondering God's love expressed in Isaiah 43 (God's calling us by name and knowing us as precious), or divine compassion in Luke 15:11–32 (the story of the prodigal son and the father's mercy), or the great challenge in Matthew 16:24–26 (the invitation to carry our cross), the soul is transformed and renewed.

Still others find the ordinary experiences of everyday life the best entrance into the presence of God. These individuals give thanks for the daily gifts of bread and time and family; they ask forgiveness in periods of injury and hurt; they petition the Lord to assist all those in trouble and in need; they praise the mystery of God in moments of special revelation.

There are still other sources of prayer, and one is poetry, which provides a rich mine for personal and communal contemplation. This series attempts to invite more and more people to use verse as a way of hearing and responding to God's voice.

Poetry has enriched my faith life not only by providing me with theological insights but also by being a major resource for personal prayer. Time and time again I have reflected on Gerard Manley Hopkins' sonnet "God's Grandeur" which contains major aspects of our faith life: creation, the fall, the restoration in the Holy Spirit. Take a few moments to read and reread this marvelous verse, to pray and re-pray this profound hymn:

> The world is charged with the grandeur of God.
> It will flame out, like shining from shook foil;
> It gathers to a greatness, like the ooze of oil
> Crushed. Why do men then now not reck his rod?
>
> Generations have trod, have trod, have trod;
> And all is seared with trade; bleared,

smeared with toil;
And wears man's smudge and
shares man's smell: the soil
Is bare now, nor can foot feel, being shod.

And for all this, nature is never spent;
There lives the dearest freshness
deep down things;
And though the last lights off
the black West went
Oh, morning, at the brown brink eastward,
springs—
Because the Holy Ghost over the bent
World broods with warm breast and with ah!
bright wings.[1]

Or take George Herbert's "Trinity Sunday." In just nine lines we receive a vision of our triune God as creator, redeemer, and sanctifier; a God who purges us of our sins, a God who encourages us to run, rise, and rest in the divine presence. This great Anglican poet captures in three stanzas what has taken some theologians over three hundred pages to articulate. Again, pause and plunge into the deep mysteries that this poet tasted so often:

Lord, who hast formed me out of mud,
And hast redeemed me through thy blood,
And sanctified me to do good;

Purge all my sins done heretofore:
For I confess my heavy score,
And I will strive to sin no more.

Enrich my heart, mouth, hands in me,
With faith, with hope, with charity;
That I may run, rise, rest with thee.[2]

Jessica Powers, the subject of this volume, is yet another poet who combines prayer and poetry in a happy marriage. Her gift of writing verse was not simply an end, but a means she used to praise and glorify God. When she began to put together her selected poetry she insisted that the volume begin and end with the focus on God. Here is her concluding poem entitled "Doxology":

God fills my being to the brim
with floods of His immensity.
I drown within a drop of Him
whose sea-bed is infinity.

The Father's will is everywhere
for chart and chance His precept keep.
There are no beaches to His care
nor cliffs to pluck from His deep.

The Son is never far away from me
for presence is what love compels.
Divinely and incarnately
He draws me where His mercy dwells.

And lo, myself am the abode
of Love, the third of the Triune,
the primal surge and sweep of God
and my eternal claimant soon!

Praise to the Father and the Son
and to the Spirit! May I be,
O Water, Wave and Tide in One,
Thine animate doxology.

(191)

It is obvious that poets like Hopkins, Herbert, and
Powers are expressing aspects of their prayer life for us.
They have spent serious time attending to God in their
life. What they saw, heard, and experienced, they shared
in poetic form. We, many years after, have the opportu-

nity of experiencing the mystery of God through their words. This dialogue is no easy task; it demands concentration and discipline.

The relationship between prayer and poetry has a long history going all the way back to the Psalms. In them, we find a variety of poetic responses to encounters with God. Down through the ages, other songs have been sung to this same end. It is fitting that this series on poetry as prayer continues that long tradition, for poems can be doors to the sacred giving us entrance into the marvelous mystery of God.

Editor's Note:

The reference numbers of Jessica Powers' poems that are used in this volume, cite the page number where the poems may be found in *The Selected Poetry of Jessica Powers*, edited by Regina Siegfried, ASC and Robert F. Morneau, and published by ICS Publications, 2131 Lincoln Road, NE, Washington DC, 20002; copyright 1999.

Chapter 1

Why Poetry? Seven "Because's"

People can survive without love; people can survive without poetry. But perhaps survival is not what human life is all about. Our dignity and nobility as human beings reside in the land of love, knowledge, and freedom—not mere existence. We are not created to focus our attention on the quantity of our years, but rather the quality of our spiritual life, not on making it through life, but rather on getting something from life and contributing our gift to the common good.

Why poetry? Why music? Why art? Indeed, why love and knowledge? Because we hunger and thirst for deep things, things like truth and goodness and beauty. These noble "transcendentals" enrich our lives and call us to fullness of being. There is a type of poverty that rivals destruction, the loss of beauty that shrinks the soul and diminishes our magnanimity. Just as the mind hungers for truth and the will for the good, so too the soul yearns for the beautiful. One of the major illnesses of our times is the divorce between faith and the arts.[1]

Poetry entered my life somewhat late, when I was in my early thirties. Indeed, along the educational road I had brief encounters with poets in high school and college—a Shakespearean sonnet, Robert Frost's "The Road Not Taken," Emily Dickinson's "I'm Nobody"—but these brief encounters ended with minimal appreciation and a lack of appropriation. A serious entanglement with poetry began, and has continued, only after I met several lovers of poetry who, through happy contagion (*felix culpa*), infected me with a love for words and the marvelous sense and sound flowing from the poetic world. I am forever addicted and I hope to spread the fire.

I offer seven "because's" to the question "Why poetry?" not as a rational demonstration of poetry's inherent worth, but as seven "reasons" that keep me in the land of poetry. Although I no longer have to be convinced of the value of verse, most people have not come to devote a portion of their energy and time to reading poetry. In fact, statistics indicate that less than five percent of the population does so on a regular basis. May these seven "because's" increase that percentage a point or two.

Because 1

"Poetry helps us to see and thus experience life more deeply."

And the poets, on whose shoulders the future rests, might, late nights, thinking things over, begin to see some meanings that elude the rest of us. —Lewis Thomas[2]

Gerard Manley Hopkins pleads: "Look at the stars! look, look up at the skies! / O look at all the fire-fold sitting in the air!" ("The Starlight Night").[3] And in his "Hurrahing in Harvest" he laments: "These things, these things were here and but the beholder / Wanting."[4] Blindness is more than the absence of 20/20 vision. Blindness is walking on a summer's night and not noticing the star-studded sky; blindness is holding a baby in one's arms and failing to appreciate the pink cheeks, the fuzzy hair, the tiny toes; blindness is being inattentive to the fresh yellow of a springtime willow, the blueness of an August sky, the industry of an ant. Poets have the capacity for keen observation. They see more things, and see them more deeply than most of us.

Coming into contact with expert "see-ers" we begin to connect with creation and taste the joy and beauty of that intimacy. Poets aid us in fostering a spirituality of presence that leads to union and to a unity that abates our loneliness and isolation. Were we to consult a spiritual optometrist, most of us would be amazed at how much assistance we need to see better and more deeply.

Jessica Powers observed life with reverence and awe. Though a small woman in stature, she stood on tiptoe and peered lovingly into God's creation. Listen to her stirring verse "Everything Rushes, Rushes":

EVERYTHING RUSHES, RUSHES

The brisk blue morning whisked in
with a thought:
everything in creation rushes, rushes
toward God—tall trees, small bushes,
quick birds and fish, the beetles round as naught,

eels in the water, deer on forest floor,
what sits in trees, what burrows underground,
what wriggles to declare life must abound,
and we, the spearhead that run on before,

and lesser things to which life cannot come:
our work, our words that move toward the Unmoved,
whatever can be touched, used, handled, loved—
all, all are rushing on *ad terminum*.

So I, with eager voice and news-flushed face,
cry to those caught in comas, stupors, sleeping:
come, everything is running,
flying,
leaping,
hurtling through time!

And we are in this race.

(163)

Someone once said that spirituality is simple to define, it's just a matter of "staying awake." Poets are people who are awake enough to see elk and deer, beetles and bushes. They also are good listeners as the morning offers the thought that all creation rushes toward God. More, poets have an eager voice, inviting us into this wonderful race, attempting to wake those who are sleeping or in a stupor. Artists have a vision and can transform our lives.

Because 2

"Poetry enlarges our world and carries us to new lands."

In one pocket of my coat I carried Tennyson's selected lyrics, and in the other, Browning's. It was as though they cast a spell of invulnerability about me. And in the darkest moments, with painful wrists and aching back, there was the precious secret of my beloved great little book. —John G. Neihardt[5]

Time and space hem us in. We are born into a certain historical era and our geography denies us physical bilocation. But poetry, engaging the memory and imagination, can draw us back to Eden's garden, to the crowning of Charlemagne, to the first landing on the moon. Poetry has the power to transport us across oceans and deserts, exhilaration and depression, success and failure, into geographies never dreamt of. Poets are tour guides pointing now to the glories of Rome, then to the smile of the Mona Lisa. If we accept their invitation to travel, our souls will expand and our narrow parochialism will diminish.

One reason for *National Geographic's* popularity is the opportunity it offers to learn about distant countries, exotic birds, etc. While staying at home the reader can journey around the planet and out into space, to discover for oneself the latest research of scientist or naturalist. The purchase of an anthology of poetry is also a passport to new experiences. Our horizons are extended as we ponder Dante's *The Divine Comedy* or read Thomas Gray's "Elegy Written in a Country Churchyard" or listen to Langston Hughes' "The Negro Speaks of Rivers." We are forever changed if we attune ourselves to the inner beauty of this poetry.

In her poem "Escape," Jessica Powers demonstrates how the power of the imagination can transport us to new geographies and lift our spirit into a larger world:

Escape

I have escaped from fear and loneliness
when this great city's dusk descends on me.
It is a childhood's game of make-believe,
filched from the years in my necessity.

I think: if I should open this dark door,
I could step into roadways lined with clover,
take the wind's merchandise of down and scent,
and have the whole starred sky of home for cover.

I think: if I would lift this window now
and pause to listen, leaning on this sill,
I might hear, for my heart's full consolation
the whip-poor-wills on some Wisconsin hill.

(102)

Poetry is a matter of opening the closed doors of our smallness and lifting high the windows sealed against the intrusions of life. It might well be that we will hear the whippoorwill or see the distress of the poor, or find the thrill and consolation of some lost love. Poetry has power to change our lives; it has transformative power to change our fears and loneliness.

Because 3

"Poetry employs metaphors and analogies that can transform our lives."

It is the experience that they stun us with, speaking it out in poetry which transcends all other languages in its power to open the doors of the heart. —Frederick Buechner[6]

Images have power. They shape our inner dispositions and affect our decision making and lifestyle. A single image can nourish us for months, even years. In Chapter 15 of John's Gospel, Jesus gives us the vine/branch analogy that captures the intimate relationship between God and human beings, a relationship of mutuality and interdependence, which brings forth life. Robert Frost's metaphor of the less traveled road continues, generation after generation, to capture a universal truth: the need we have to make limited decisions in a world of seemingly unlimited possibilities.

In "I'm Nobody," Emily Dickinson raises the issue of human dignity and notoriety. Symbols, images, metaphors, analogies change our lives. The theologian Avery Dulles offers this "job description" of symbols and images: "Symbols transform the horizons of man's life, integrate his perception of reality, alter his scale of values, reorient his loyalties, attachments, and aspirations in a manner far exceeding the powers of abstract conceptual thought."[7]

In his book, *The Broken Connection*, Robert Jay Lifton speaks about the relationship of images, attitudes, and behavior. The argument runs quite simply: we live on images; images lead to attitudes; attitudes lead to behavior. Thus, if we are desirous of changing our behavior, it is insufficient to simply change our attitude. We must go deeper and change our images of God, self, the world—everything. Poetry participates in the quest for a culture based on beauty, not ugliness. Metaphor is a primary means in this struggle.

Jessica Powers is a master of metaphor. In "The Tear in the Shade" the poet cleverly links obsessive guilt with the way a small mishap can be magnified in one's mind:

The Tear in the Shade

I tore the new pale window shade with slightly
more than a half-inch tear.
I knew the Lady would be shocked to see
what I had done with such finality.
I went outside to lose my worry there.
Later when I came back into the room
it seemed that nothing but the tear was there.

There had been furniture, a rug, and pictures,
and on the table flowers in purple bloom.
It was amazing how they dwindled, dwindled,
and how the tear grew till it filled the room.

(118)

Many of us have had the experience of over-identifying with a specific weakness or fault in our lives. We lose perspective, unable to see the large picture, the tear—this sin, that weakness, this characteristic—is everything. How clearly the poet captures our dilemma and names for us a reality that often leads to discouragement and possibly despair. But here is the beauty of the poetic gifts:

the truth of this poem is that life is larger than any tear, that we need not be consumed by a preoccupation with self. Our self-importance leads to excessive introspection. Poetic truth can lead to genuine freedom.

Because 4

"Poetry assists prose in helping language reach its full potential."

Whilst thus the poet animates nature with his own thoughts, he differs from the philosopher only herein, that the one proposes Beauty as his main end; the other Truth.
—Ralph Waldo Emerson[8]

Prose has a hard time flying. The gravity of literalism holds it close to the earth, though flight *is* possible when such graced masters as Newman, Dickens or Jefferson set pen to paper. By its very nature, prose informs, whereas poetry, freed from the shackles of scientific truth or perhaps historical truth, is able to suggest, hint, observe, and even conceal a whole range of human experiences. The obituary in the daily newspaper reads quite differently from John Donne's "Death Be Not Proud." Language can invite us to dance as well as walk, and poets facilitate the rhythm of language.

While we do not want pilots and control tower personnel to be speaking poetic language, hopefully we do not limit human discourse to literal meanings. Prose cannot always capture the many-layered world of affection. Prose is not always able to articulate sufficiently the glory of a sunset or the tragic death of a loved one. Another language system is needed to appeal to the emotions as much as to the mind. Poets and philosophers and scientists are necessary if we are to be given a full picture of reality. The lack of any one of these voices leaves us impoverished.

Once, while spending a day in the infirmary, Jessica Powers turned a time of illness into a thing of beauty, and made language dance.

Siesta in Color

Near a glazed window drinking south and west
in thirst of sunlight in the early spring,
I with a sudden luck of illness take
magic siesta. I commune with color,
hobnob with rainbows on the coasts of slumber,
revisit prisms of long disregard.

Soft pinks, impetuous yellows splash the wall

and line my eyelids as I drift toward sleep;
blue, green and aqua prance in patterns; purple
and lavender to squares and circles run.
I think if I could track this charm to source
or else to terminal I might discover
opening or dropoff or amazing shore
to color's primal meaning.
                              Yet I muse:
is not pure fact a fullness? I remember
how rainbows had addressed me as a child,
how light and color made their language heard.
Though I was not yet judge or analyst,
something secure was given, kept; I held,
as with my grandmother's warm bursts of Gaelic,
sweet words that had no meaning but were there.

(76)

The poet could have chosen another language system to describe her experience: "Last week I spent a day in the infirmary where I watched the southwest sun pour colors into the room. I tried, without success, to trace all that beauty to its source. While fighting sleep a thought occurred to me that maybe it didn't make any difference.

Beauty in and of itself has its own justification. Facts sometimes do not need to be plundered for their meaning. My Gaelic grandmother spoke to me in a language I did not understand, but it was still delightful and brought me a sense of security." When prose comes up against poetry, there really is no contest.

Because 5

"Poetry, written or read in faith, can be a form of deep prayer."

Poetry ever goes like the royal banners before ascending life; therefore, man may safely follow its leadership in his prayer, which is—or should be—life in its intensest form.
—Evelyn Underhill[9]

Access to God comes in many forms. God speaks to us through the gift of revelation in Sacred Scripture; God is encountered in creation and in the ambiguities of nature; God is experienced in the sacraments and the teaching of the undivided Church. And, yes, God speaks to us and elicits our response through artists, indeed, through poets. Poets mediate moments of grace and draw their readers into their sensed experience. Poets in every century have used their skill to articulate moments of contemplation and have thereby given their readers access to much of the beauty and truth that lodged in their poetic souls.

Central both to the life of prayer and to the life of a poet is the quality of "loving attention." To be present with deep respect and concern gives us entry into vast fields of reality. Some of the mystics called contemplation, which is one of the deepest forms of prayer, nothing other than "loving attention." Poets, too, have an amazing capacity for insight, the ability to stare, to look at reality in all its glory and horror. From that attentive perspective, they capture their vision both in sense and sound.

Jessica Powers experienced the "nowness" and "hereness" of God. Moreover, she was gifted with the ability to describe her experience and invite others into the sacred Presence. Enter now into the heart of this contemplative poet.

GOD IS TODAY

> God is today.
> He is not yesterday.
> He is not tomorrow.
>
> God is the dawn, wakening earth to life;

the first morning ever,
shining with infinite innocence; a revelation
older than all beginning, younger than youth.
God is the noon, blinding the eye of the mind
with the blaze of truth.
God is the sunset, casting over creation
a color of glory
as He withdraws into mysteries of light.

God is today.
He is not yesterday.
He is not tomorrow.
He never is night.

(13)

Though poetry is not theology, in this verse there are
many claims regarding the nature of God. We experience
God primarily in the "now," neither focusing on the past
nor anxiously gazing toward the future. God is the one
who awakens us *now*, who gives us truth in the noonday
sun *now*, who shares divine glory in the evening beauties
of creation *now*. God is light, not darkness or night. This
poem arose out of prayer, and when pondered in the quiet
of our own hearts, can lead to great praise and joy.

Because 6

"Poetry helps us to name experiences and feelings that are often illusive and ambiguous."

The task of the poet is to make clear to himself, and thereby to others, the temporal and eternal questions. —Ibsen[10]

What we are unable to name controls us. This is especially true of that wide range of emotions that cascade through our minds and hearts. Be they fears or anxieties, be they worries or desires, we strive to recognize the multiple dimensions of our rich interiority. Psychology is a helpful science that offers a lexicon of theories to assist us in self-knowledge and in the knowledge of others. But even the sciences come up short in dealing with the mysteries of the inner domain.

Poets have a special skill in "naming the nameless." At least, they provide sketches and analogies to draw us close to a knowledge of our inner workings. Naming is not so much a matter of control and domination as it is a desire to understand and appreciate the complexities of our life. We thirst for genuine knowledge and we long to be able to communicate with others whatever is transpiring deep within. The poet aids us in this process by giving us a language to describe profound, universal human experiences.

Jessica Powers knew fear—imagined and real. In her later wisdom she realized that the real battles of life are more internal than external.

OLD BRIDGE

Here is the bridge my childhood marked with fear.
I thought an ogre waited under it,
quick to devour if I should venture near.
I ran at sight of it; my sandals hit

the brown dust of the roadway going by.
Oh, it was like a day of lifted dread
when I grew bold enough to peer and pry,
seeking the monster, finding peace instead.

Fled is that childish fear; my thoughts are couched
in grown-up wisdom now, and yet I find
that worse than ogres are the dark shapes crouched
lurking beneath the bridges of my mind.

(104)

All of us have our bridges that we must pass over as we continue our journey of life. What lurks beneath them we can only conjecture. Ahab had his white whale; King David, his inner demons. The apostles too faced many trials on their road of discipleship. Interestingly, looking fear in the eye often drives it off running. Many are the false (non-existent) fears that paralyze our days. The poet names her fears for us and challenges us to do the same.

Because 7

"Poetry provides another human voice to let us know we are not alone."

It is difficult to imagine Grandmother having to respond to the great moments of her life without all that poetry that she and Augusta had read together. —Wallace Stegner[11]

Few mistakes are worse than traveling alone. As social beings we need one another at every level of our being. We need physical touch, psychological reassurance, spiritual mentoring. The poets speak words of wisdom and consolation, challenge and confrontation. For every season and for every occasion, a poet stands up and shares a perspective. We may not agree; we may feel threatened.

But at least we have someone speaking to the situation after careful reflection.

During the Christmas season we may turn to T. S. Eliot and read "The Journey of the Magi." The poet ponders the difference between birth and death, the worthwhileness of the journey. When assessing what we are doing with our lives, we do well to listen to the Spanish poet Antonio Machado who asks what we have done and are doing to the garden entrusted to each of us. If we are struggling with the question of love, we have a whole battalion of poets ranging from Dante to Elizabeth Barrett Browning to William Shakespeare and, yes, Jessica Powers, eager to speak their minds on the issues.

Listen to Powers sing of the great grace of love:

THE GIFT OF LOVE

> My thoughts of you are fair as precious stones
> out of the memory's deep mysterious mines.
> I cut and polish, hold the gems to light—
> color of sea water, color of wines
> coaxed from the earth's sweetest fruits.
> I drop them down

into my heart, into the lifted hands
of love whose lone concern is your renown.

(52)

We find here none of the modern romanticism that
sees love primarily in terms of self-satisfaction. Rather,
the whole thrust of the love described here is the well-
being of the other. It flows from a care for the other,
thoughts like gems that sparkle with the beloved's at-
tributes. Here love is concern, and, let us add, respect
and responsibility. It is a love residing deep in the heart
where it is held with tender care.

All poets have a "cause" (indeed, a number of
"because's") behind their vocation. Glancing into the
verse of my favorite ten poets, of whom Jessica Powers is
one, I offer these suggestions as answers to the question:
"Why Poetry?":

Why Poetry? Ten "Because's"

From Amherst & Ms. Dickinson:
"Because my vocation is to sing."

From Paris & Master Rilke:
"Because someone must speak for the caged
panther."

From Bemerton & Pastor Herbert:
"Because my soul needs words for praise."

From Gidding & T. S. Eliot:
"Because the Magi must their story tell."

From New Hampshire & Robert Lee Frost:
"Because roads taken, untaken, make all the difference."

From Wales & Gerard Manley Hopkins:
"Because dappled things are glorious."

From Madrid & Antonio Machado:
"Because dreams reveal an indwelling God."

From Pewaukee & Jessica Powers:
"Because the heart would burst without expression."

From London & William Shakespeare:
"Because true love does not alter with alteration."

From the Lake District & William Wordsworth:
"Because daffodils long to sing."

(Robert F. Morneau)

23

CHAPTER 2

The Poet — Jessica Powers

A Quiet Life

There are different ways of entering a person's life. Knowledge of Jesus comes to us through the writings of the early Christian communities by way of the various gospel accounts. We learn about Abraham Lincoln or Harry Truman by tracing their political campaigns, presidential decisions, and personal letters. Other individuals are harder to know because their lives are less public, less "eventful." Yet, their stories may well be no less intriguing nor less deserving of preservation.

Biographer Dana Greene comments on her subject, Evelyn Underhill:

Evelyn Underhill's life was "quiet"; it was not marked by adventurous acts and deeds. Although her life circumstances are important in that they provide... the raw data for her development, a biography that focused on them rather than on the development of her mind and spirit would miss the meaning of her life. The adventure here is the inner one, the conflict and reconciliation of mind and heart, the development of individual consciousness and its ultimate transcendence.[1]

Such is also the case with the Carmelite poet Jessica Powers. Her external life was devoid of high drama. Rather, it was her rich interior life as a committed religious, and her dedication to the art of poetry, that are the defining features of her personality. Before venturing into her poetry as a source of prayer, we do well to spend some time reflecting on various questions: Who were the important people in her life? What factors and forces shaped her thinking and emotions? What role did God play in her life? Why did she become a religious and what did community life mean to her?

Key People in Jessica Powers' Life

On February 7, 1905, Jessica Powers (baptismal record: Agnes Jessika Powers) was born to John Powers (1865–1918) and Delia Trainer Powers (1867–1925). Her birthplace was the rural farming community known as Cat Tail Valley, located several miles from the small city of Mauston, in the western part of Wisconsin. Her father's parents were from County Waterford, Ireland. Her maternal grandfather, James Trainer, came from Scotland, and through him, the Powers family linked their history to the Scottish poet, Robert Burns.

Jessica Powers was one of four children. She had an older sister, Catherine Dorothy (1899–1916), who died of tuberculosis at the age of 17, and two brothers, John Trainer (1901–1977) and James Daniel (1906–1956). The influence her Scottish-Irish family had on Jessica cannot be overestimated. The atmosphere was one of Roman Catholic tradition, a reverence and love for the land, a mixture of humor and melancholy. In her poetic musings, one can feel the deep influence of her Christian family wherein faith played a central role.

A significant person in Jessica Powers' early life was the Dominican religious, Sister Lucille Massart. While attending the parish school in Mauston, Jessica began writing at Sister Lucille's encouragement. This perceptive religious saw great potential in her young student and fostered the development of Jessica's creative talent. Such encouragement can be the turning point in a person's life; we are often blind to our own gifts and hidden potential, and it takes an outside mentor to confirm a talent and to ignite the fire that gets it burning. This may well have been the case with Jessica Powers.

Two other people had an effect on Jessica's creativity, the neo-Thomist philosopher Anton Pegis and his wife Jessie. Between 1937 and 1941, Jessica Powers lived with the Pegis family in New York. It was in this home that Jessica Powers and Jessie Pegis shared poetry, enjoyed many evenings of passionate conversation about philosophy and life, and deepened a friendship that would last for years. Living in New York also provided Jessica with an opportunity for membership in the Catholic Poetry Society of America, and in 1939, Jessica published her first book of verse, *The Lantern Burns*.

Anton and Jessie Pegis had two children who became the object of Jessica Powers' special affection. Because Jessica was a poet with a highly developed sense of seeing and hearing, the Pegis children provided her with much material for poetic reflection. In a real sense, the Pegis family became Jessica's family through their friendship and hospitality.

In glancing through my personal correspondence from Jessica Powers, I came across a number of other individuals she mentioned specifically as people who uniquely touched her life. She named the poets Walt Whitman, e. e. cummings, Mark Van Doren, Edna St. Vincent Millay, and George Herbert; the editor of her own poetry, Sister Regina Seigfried, ASC, and her biographer, Dolores Leckey; her priest cousin, Father Bernard McCarty; her dear friend Sister Eileen Surles of the Cenacle; the great mystic Saint John of the Cross and the theologian Johannes Metz. And the list goes on. Jessica's life was shaped and influenced either through personal contact or by reading the works of these great poets and authors.

In her thirties, Jessica became a Carmelite religious and remained one until her death forty-seven years later. The joys and sorrows, the ups and downs of living in close proximity for many years, often causes a bonding among women religious that defies measurement. And this was the case in Jessica Powers' life. Together, the members of her Carmelite community prayed, studied, ate, rejoiced, and suffered. As Jessica's "primary community," her sisters were major shapers of her mind and heart.

Jessica's life was one of faith. God was the central mystery of her life, and it was the reality of the Trinity and the Incarnation that most influenced her thought and affections. Her relationship to the Father as Creator, to Jesus as Redeemer and Friend, to the Holy Spirit as fire and Deifier shows us the true identity of Jessica, poet and religious. She nurtured her relationship with God over the years through prayer and study, fasting and discipline, service and love. As one reads the poems of this religious, it becomes obvious that the mysteries of faith took up residence in the center of her heart.

Key Moments

Within all our lives there are specific stepping stones, decisive moments that shape and define our character, indeed, our destiny. These crossroad experiences help us to express our values and carry us into the future. Several of Jessica Powers' crossroads were sacramental moments that reveal something of this poet's mind and heart.

Jessica Powers was baptized at Saint Patrick's Church in Mauston, Wisconsin, on February 26, 1905; she made her first Holy Communion at age 13 in 1918, and was confirmed the following year. Underlying these grace-giving events was Jessica's immersion in the mystery of faith, the conviction that God's redeeming love is present and active in life. Jessica grew up in a faith environment that gave a central place to religious belief and practice. Her intellect, heart, and imagination were imbued with the Catholic way of life from a very early age.

In 1922, Jessica Powers enrolled at Marquette University in Milwaukee. Since women were not allowed in the liberal arts school at that time, she registered under the school of journalism. However, after only one semester at Marquette, she was forced to return home due to the high cost of education.

Jessica remained on the family farm for a short time and then moved to Chicago to work in a secretarial pool. Jessica loved the big city's energy and excitement, and she was able to spend considerable time browsing through local libraries. In Chicago, Jessica joined a poetry group at the River Forest Dominican Priory, and her own skill at writing poetry was greatly refined. She began dreaming of going to New York to pursue a literary career.

In 1924, however, Jessica showed signs of tuberculosis, which had already taken the life of her sister eight years before. She returned to the farm for medical treatment, which seemed successful. Then, on September 12, 1925, her mother died suddenly. Jessica's two unmarried brothers were left to manage the farm, and Jessica resigned herself to caring for them and for the farmhouse.

Two outstanding qualities emerge from these years: Jessica Powers' deep love for learning, especially her love of literature, and her self-sacrificing spirit. Having tasted big city life with all of its stimuli and intellectually broadening experiences, Jessica's return to rural Wisconsin and the routine of farm life provided moments of real challenge. Years later, Jessica remembered the period as desolate, but her poetry of that period shows how she allowed life's circumstances to hone her inner spirit. It was during these years that Jessica began to submit various poems she had been working on, both to local papers and to *The Milwaukee Sentinel*.

In 1936, both brothers married, and Jessica wrote to a friend that she now felt "free to fly away." She went first to Chicago, and then boarded a Greyhound bus for New York, with no job prospects, no contacts, and very little money. Perhaps the urgency of finally following her dreams gave Jessica the courage, determination, and sense of adventure needed for such a step.

Once in New York, Jessica immediately joined the Catholic Poetry Society. There, she met Eileen Surles who introduced her to the Sisters of the Cenacle, and Jessica Powers began to make regular retreats at the Cenacle Retreat House. It was during one of these retreats that the course of her life would change once more—this time, most dramatically.

In 1940, Jessica attended the Cenacle retreat led by Jesuit priest Charles Connors. In a personal conversation with her, Connors asked her how she envisioned spending the rest of her life. Jessica Powers responded that her deepest desire was to be a Carmelite, but she knew this was impossible because of her lack of funds and her poor health. Besides, she reasoned, at 35, she was far past the usual age for embracing such a rigorous path. Connors advised that she would never know if she could live the life until she gave it a try; and he cautioned her against drifting through life with no real purpose.

Jessica must have thought and prayed deeply over his words during the retreat days that followed. Up to that time she had experienced many things: the enriching friendship of the Pegis family; the give and take among members of a poetry society; the invaluable resources of numerous public libraries; being frequently published in magazines, literary journals and newspapers. In fact, Jessica was at that moment on the very cusp of literary success with the publication of her first book of poetry, titled *The Lantern Burns*.

These had been years of rich educational, religious, literary, and cultural growth. Certainly, the risk entailed in leaving the life she had built for herself was not lost on Jessica. But, once more, Jessica's adventurous spirit led the way. She wrote to a new Carmelite monastery still under construction in her home state. And she was accepted. Jessica Powers was to become a Carmelite nun.

Jessica entered the Carmel of the Mother of God in Milwaukee in 1941, and she remained a member of that community until her death on August 18, 1988—a total of forty-seven years. On April 25, 1942, her "clothing day" as a Carmelite, she took the religious name Sister Miriam of the Holy Spirit, and on May 8, 1945, Jessica made her first profession of vows. One year later she made her perpetual profession.

In 1955, Jessica was elected prioress. She guided the relocation of the monastery from downtown Milwaukee to Pewaukee, an area west of the city. Jessica served a second term as prioress from 1958–1961, and yet another term from 1964–1967. The only significant interruption of her life in Carmel was the year she spent at a tuberculosis sanatorium from October 1959 to October 1960.

Jessica Power's forty-seven years as a Carmelite were filled with liturgical and private prayer, rigorous fasting and discipline, the joys and struggles of community life, the writing of poetry, correspondence with friends, walks in nature, household chores. As a religious, Jessica dedicated herself to a life of poverty, chastity, and obedience. She pondered the Word of God and celebrated the Eucharist thousands and thousands of times. Her poetry hints at a personal knowledge of the dark night of the senses and the spirit. Her special love for the Holy Spirit is evidenced both in her poetry and in her personality traits of humor and joy which radiated from the working of the Spirit in her soul.

We do not have access to other, more interior decisions which Jessica Powers made on a daily basis. Some of these were certainly difficult as she exercised her authority as prioress in the turbulent 1960s. Other daily decisions involving her various ways of celebrating life were perhaps easier. Like all of us, some days were more successful than others. But her central choice was to listen attentively and respond wholeheartedly to the ways of God.

Personal Reflection

In the summer of 1985, I was teaching a course on spirituality at Saint Norbert College in De Pere, Wisconsin. Several times during the sessions, I referred to poetry and its power to shape and influence our imagination, indeed, our spiritual life. After one class, a student came up and asked if I knew the poet Jessica Powers. When I confessed my lack of knowledge, I was given a small volume of Jessica Powers' verse titled *The House at Rest* (published privately by the Carmel in 1984).

Busy with other things to read and do, I did not pick up *The House at Rest* until autumn. But when I did, I was astounded at the poetry's quality. The clarity of the verse, its simplicity, its insight, its rootedness in nature and grace—all this lead me to call the monastery and ask for a visit with Sister Miriam of the Holy Spirit.

Several months later we met, and continued to do so on a regular basis for the next four years. Until our first meeting, I had imagined her as one usually imagines "public" figures, people seen on TV, heard on the radio, or read of in books. I pictured her a scholarly type, as substantial physically as she was intellectually, with a powerful and convincing manner of speaking.

But when she walked into the room, I had to reconstruct my image immediately. Jessica was a rural woman who had lived close to the soil, a small person with a soft, melodic voice. She had sparkling eyes and a trace of a smile upon her lips that hinted at her quick wit. Although her presence in the room revealed simplicity, she missed nothing that went on around her.

As I got to know her over the months and years that followed, I found Jessica Powers to be a woman thankful for her gifts, and knowledgeable of her limitations. She impressed me as an authentic person, one who loved God and life and who embraced joys and sorrows with equal gratitude.

During our first visit, I asked Sister Miriam if she had other poetry than those published in *The House at Rest*. A foolish question indeed! Tucked away were over four hundred poems, many that were unpublished. When I inquired about obtaining more, Jessica referred me to Sister Regina Siegfried, ASC, living in St. Louis. Over the years Sister Regina had been collecting Jessica's verse and carefully organizing the poetry. Eventually Sister Regina and I met with Jessica, went through the entire corpus of her work, and together we selected 183 poems that were published in *The Selected Poetry of Jessica Powers* (Sheed & Ward, 1989). The volume has gone through six reprintings, and was re-issued by ICS Publications in 1999.

Between 1985 and 1988, I corresponded with Jessica every few months. Our letters and notes were brief. We wrote about poets, current books and articles dealing with prayer and spirituality, various events going on in the life of the Church. Sensitive to the seasons, Jessica would often comment on the beauty of nature. She would also speak of community events, retreat experiences, the richness of liturgical feasts...

A Memorable Personality

Several "sets" of Jessica's personality qualities remain impressed upon my memory from my contact with her—the first set, humility and humor. Jessica Powers knew who she was: a creature of God, a rural-farm-girl-turned-religious, a person loved and gifted by God. Her humor, an expression of her rich insight and response to the incongruity of life, was always ready to explode. Though deeply serious about life, she was quick to pick up on the lightness of being, which often reveals itself in everyday life.

A second set of characteristics was her reverence for life and her sense of wonder. Poets have highly developed senses of seeing and hearing, and Jessica was no exception. People and life demand respect, and she gave it; creation deserves our awe and from Jessica it was forthcoming. One need only ponder her "nature poems" to realize that the mystery of creation and praise for the Creator were pivotal to her spirituality.

A third set of qualities I witnessed in my visits and correspondence included the importance of relationships and a heart of gratitude. Jessica was a friend before she was a poet: a friend of God, a friend of her community members, a friend of those who were privileged to enter her circle. Work and creativity were not the most important things in her life. Furthermore, her gratitude for so many gifts—family, faith, a religious vocation, poetry—was expressed day after day at the altar. The Eucharistic Celebration was for her the centerpiece of her spiritual and personal life. It was there that she gave God thanks and praise for all that she was and all she had been given.

I will share one story that reveals a great deal of her unpretentious character. As we were nearing the completion of her volume of selected poetry, I contacted an artist in Milwaukee. I gave the artist several photographs of Jessica and asked her to compose a large pencil sketch of the poet. Several months later the sketch was complete, and the resemblance was striking. I brought it to the monastery to show Jessica, who was not pleased. Her displeasure, however, was certainly not over the quality of the work, but over the fact that she had been the subject of such a work at all. I remember leaving the monastery with the sketch and no small feeling of embarrassment. I needed no further evidence to confirm for myself that Jessica was graced with the virtue of humility.

Jessica's Self-Metaphor: The Sparrow

THE LEGEND OF THE SPARROW

(For a child who dreams of sainthood)

There was a sparrow once who dreamed to fly into
the sun.
Oh, how the birds of earth set up a cry
at such imprudence in a little one
when even eagles dared not venture near
the burning stratosphere.

"She will come down within a mile or two,"
they prophesied with dread.
It was, of course, most pitifully true.
Scarce half-way up the mountain overhead
she crashed into her feathers, as they said.

But when her wings healed, up she shot again
and sought a further bough.
She was more humble and more cautious now,
after a brief novitiate of pain.

Three times she rose; twice the wind brought her
down,
once her own weariness.

At last she clutched a branch in her distress
and cried, "How can I ever hope to rest
in the sun's downy nest?
I faint; I fall whatever way I go!"

But then she turned and saw the home she left
unnumbered miles below,
while just beyond her lay the mountain top,
a kerchiefed head of snow.

Nobody told her and she never guessed
that earth's last height was all that she need seek.
All winds blow upward from the mountain peak
and there the sun has such magnetic rays
that in one moment she was lifted up
into his tender blaze.

Down in the valley there was such a stir:
A sparrow reached the sun!
Why had the wind and weather favored her?
What had she ever done?
Yet since they must, they spoke the praising word,
measured her flight and paused to gasp afresh.
What was she really but a little bird,
all feather and no flesh?

Only the sun knew, and the moving air
the miracle thereof:
a bird that wings itself with resolute love
can travel anywhere.

(4–5)

Jessica Powers had many identities: creature, child of
God, daughter, sister, religious, friend, poet, a "Wiscon-
sin Emily Dickinson," a woman of the twentieth century.
The self-metaphor of the sparrow expressed her personal
identity as she saw it: a rather humble, non-colorful bird
seeking God. The image of an eagle simply would not fit
her self-identity, and certainly not the proud, strutting
peacock. Nor would the wise owl or swift hummingbird
be appropriate. A sparrow—a simple, lowly, brown spar-
row—provided a symbol both in size and connotation to
describe this religious woman who sought to fly into the
heights of God's love.

So often, poets find analogies in nature to articulate
their most profound feelings. And other birds, about
which Jessica wrote, give us clues regarding other aspects
of her personality. She writes of the killdeers ("Like Kill-
deers Crying," 184) and their wild despair, their lonely
cries; Jessica was no stranger to the deep human experi-

ences of loss with its consequent emotions. The death of family members, her departure from friends in New York, the inevitable dry periods of prayer that all contemplatives have to face, led Jessica to identify with the killdeer's cry in the night.

Jessica returns to the image of a sparrow in "Poet of a Gentler Time":

> On a shrill street he mourns his nightingales
> through whom love spoke; he writes in weightless verse
> his anguish at the absence of the lark.
> I come to him; I bring him rueful tales
> that the small birds of indigence rehearse
> on the bare branches of a city park.
>
> Surely, he cries, where towers make wilderness,
> and stones supplant the moss, and song gives way
> to raucous speech, you must in tears confess
> a most unmusical and loveless day.
>
> My words torment him with the prick of arrows.
> Not soon, not ever will he understand
> that love may learn the accent of the sparrows,
> having no larks or nightingales at hand.

(185)

One can taste the autobiographical flavor of these lines. Love does not demand the songs of larks and nightingales, beautiful as these are. Love does not need the action of dramatic events and spectacular displays to prove its authenticity. Small birds of indigence (sparrows) have their own accent that can turn a day, a life, into something musical and love-filled; indeed, something worthy to give glory to God. Sparrows, too, know something of doxology.

ROBIN AT DUSK

I can go starved the whole day long,
draining a stone, eating a husk,
and never hunger till a song
breaks from a robin's throat at dusk.

I am reminded only then
how far from day and human speech,
how far from the loud world of men
lies the bright dream I strain to reach.

Oh, that a song of mine could burn
the air with beauty so intense,
sung with a robin's unconcern
for any mortal audience!

Perhaps I shall learn presently
his secret when the shadows stir,
and I shall make one song and be
aware of but one Listener.

(187)

Along with the sparrow, Jessica identifies herself with
the small robin. She yearns to learn the secret of the robin
and its "unconcern for any mortal audience." She almost
envies the intense beauty of the robin's evening song,
one that is sung to but one Listener. The poet here cares
nothing about a human audience, but only wants her song
to be heard by God, whom she longs to be conscious of
and united to. The poet's business is to sing, and for Jessica Powers it mattered not if there was but one member
in the audience.

Jessica's God: Lover

God's attribute of love may seem strange to a contemporary world that emphasizes the romantic, courtship
side of love. But those who are trained in discipleship,
and who embrace the invitation to the cross, experience
love as essentially self-giving. Such love is death to oneself for the sake of life. It is a total giving which emulates
the mystery of God's self-donation in Jesus.

Jessica Powers continuously pondered the mystery of this strange Lover in her life. Her experience of the cross was part of the "package deal" of Christianity, a sharing in the Paschal Mystery. For her, the cloistered life was not an escape into an ethereal, immune milieu, free from the trials and stresses of daily life, but rather another step on the path of following Jesus wherever he leads. Ultimately, it was Jesus who revealed to her the mystery of God. And what stranger ways are there than that of Bethlehem and Calvary?

God Is a Strange Lover

God is the strangest of all lovers; His ways are past explaining.
He sets His heart on a soul: He says to Himself, "Here will I rest my love."
But He does not woo her with flowers or jewels or words that are set to music,
no names endearing, no kindled praise His heart's direction prove.
His jealousy is an infinite thing. He stalks the soul with sorrows;
He tramples the bloom; He blots the sun that could make her vision dim.

He robs and breaks and destroys—there is nothing
at last but her
own shame, her own affliction,
and then He comes and there is nothing in the vast
world but Him and her love of Him.

Not till the great rebellions die and her will is safe
in His hands forever
does He open the door of light and His
tendernesses fall, and then for what is seen in the
soul's virgin places,
for what is heard in the heart, there is no speech at all.

God is a strange lover; the story of His love
is most surprising.
There is no proud queen in her cloth of gold; over
and over again
there is only, deep in the soul, a poor disheveled
woman weeping...
for us who have need of a picture and words:
the Magdalen.

(16)

In October of 1997, a hundred years after the death
of Thérèse of Lisieux, and seventy-five years after her

canonization, the saint was named a doctor of the Church. The Little flower, as she was affectionately called, knew the "strangeness" of God's love. She lived the last eighteen months of her life with incredible pain of body and spirit. Amazingly, during this time of terrible darkness, she was still able to support others on their own struggling journeys. Jessica Powers knew this same God. She suffered from tuberculosis. She knew the loneliness of the human condition. She, too, tasted the dark night. And yet, she was able to sing of this strangest of all Lovers in the above poem.

Jessica writes of the cross and of suffering in other poems: "The Moment after Suffering" (87), "The Masses" (89), "I Measure Loneliness" (114). These verses are grounded in the personal experience of this Carmelite nun—a woman who confronted her own physical, psychological, and spiritual struggles as we all do, and who found herself having to deal with those of others, particularly during her time as prioress.

Jessica's God: Mercy

Roman Catholicism and the Carmelite tradition were major influences in shaping the way Jessica Powers understood God. Also influential were her experiences of creation (nature) as well as her own interior experiences of a triune God. In planning the edition of her collected works, Jessica insisted that the first poem in the volume would be "The Mercy of God," and the last poem, "Doxology." There was no doubt that her poetic gift was focused on making God known and loved.

For this poet, God had many marvelous attributes: truth ("God Is Today," 13), light ("The Vision," 2–3), presence ("This Trackless Solitude," 6), hospitality ("The Uninvited," 10), compassion and forgiveness ("Repairer of Fences," 14), generosity ("But Not With Wine," 17), vastness and infinity ("The Ledge of Light," 22). Once, when she visited an editor in New York, a discussion arose as to God's greatest attribute. The poet argued for beauty, the editor for truth. But Jessica's opinion was later entirely transformed. Shortly before her death, she commented that the greatest of God's attributes is divine mercy.

In today's world, the volume of anger and vengeance is exceedingly great. The "tit for tat" philosophy reigns in the hearts and minds of many peoples and nations. Jessica Powers reminds us that—without downplaying the need for justice—we need mercy, forgiveness, and reconciliation. How relevant are her thoughts as we enter a new millennium and are challenged to pass on to others the mercy that we ourselves have received.

Jessica knew the mercy of God and was thus able to write so profoundly about this grace. Her God was "a merciful and gracious God, slow to anger and rich in kindness and fidelity..." (Ex 34:6).

Jessica's God: Our Eternal Home

Every person has a particular way of seeing, of knowing, and of acting. The philosophical categories for these "ways" are metaphysics, epistemology, and ethics. Jessica Powers lived within the Catholic tradition which claims that our true country is with God, and that we are ultimately destined for heaven. Because of this, we often experience a feeling of homelessness during this life, a sense of being-in-exile that is intensely painful for those whose deepest yearning is for full union with God.

As a contemplative who was part of a contemplative tradition, the poet Jessica Powers spent countless hours in personal and communal prayer. The writings of the great Carmelite saints, John of the Cross and Teresa of Avila, shaped Jessica Powers' metaphysics, her way of seeing the world. She once commented that immediately upon discovering the works of John of the Cross, she thought she had died and gone to heaven. In pondering these mystical sources her homelessness temporarily diminished, for in the land and mystery of silence and solitude to which John of the Cross led her, Jessica's desire for divine union grew more and more intense.

But, all too soon, aware of the limitations of time and space and sensitive to the finiteness of her human mind and heart, Jessica felt her anguish and melancholy return to pester her soul like small birds chasing crows away from their nest. And the duties of convent life, the everyday routine, brought back those restless feelings. Jessica faced the reality that our true home is not here.

"Homelessness" does not allow for clear definition. Though it includes a lack of owning places and things, it has much more to do with matters of the heart and with the mystery of the soul. Being a stranger to love is homelessness; tasting the enigma of loneliness is homelessness; being unable to express one's inner being in fluid and free-flowing creativity is homelessness. Ultimately, homelessness lies in our inability to comprehend and possess Infinity, the mystery of God, by whom and for whom we are made. It is the incapacity for satisfying our hunger for God with temporary fulfillments. Our humanity "bumps against" divinity, and we grieve in our incomprehension. But let the poet tell it in her own words:

There is a homelessness, never to be clearly defined.
It is more than having no place of one's own,
no bed or chair.
It is more than walking in a waste of wind,
or gleaning the crumbs where someone else
has dined,
or taking a coin for food or cloth to wear.
The loan of things and the denial of things are
possible to bear.

It is more, even, than homelessness of heart,
of being always a stranger at love's side,
of creeping up to a door only to start
at a shrill voice and to plunge back to the wide
dark of one's own obscurity and hide.

It is the homelessness of the soul
in the body sown;
it is the loneliness of mystery:
of seeing oneself a leaf, inexplicable and
unknown,
cast from an unimaginable tree;

of knowing one's life to be a brief wind blown
down a fissure of time in the rock of eternity.
The artist weeps to wrench this grief from stone;
he pushes his hands through the
tangled vines of music,
but he cannot set it free.

It is the pain of the mystic suddenly thrown
back from the noon of God to the night
of his own humanity.
It is his grief; it is the grief of all those praying
in finite words to an Infinity
Whom, if they saw, they could not comprehend;
Whom they cannot see.

(86)

Jessica's God: Seen in Creation

FOR A LOVER OF NATURE

Your valley trails its beauty through your poems,
the kindly woods, the wide majestic river.
Earth is your god—or goddess, you declare,
mindful of what good time must one day give her

of all you have. Waters and rocks and trees
hold primal words born out of Genesis.

But Love is older than these.

You lay your hand upon the permanence
of green-embroidered land and miss the truth
that you are trusting your immortal spirit
to earth's sad inexperience and youth.
Centuries made this soil; this rock was lifted
out of the aeons; time could never trace
a path to water's birth or air's inception,
and so, you say, these be your godly grace.
Earth was swept into being with the light—
dear earth, you argue, who will soon be winning
your flesh and bones by a most ancient right.

But Love had no beginning.

(165)

Raised in a rural landscape, it is not surprising that
Jessica Powers had a deep love for the land. The valleys
and meadows, the rivers and lakes, the birds and the cattle,
the beloved seasons, all made their impression on the
poet's imagination. But always there was a clear distinc-

tion between the Creator and the creation, between the Giver and the gift. The earth was neither god nor goddess; all creation, by reflecting and making manifest aspects of the Creator, deserved respect, but not adoration.

Wisconsin has strong seasons. Summer and winter leave no doubt about their identity; autumn and spring, though transitional times, are unambiguous as to their calling. Jessica Powers spent all but six of her 83 years in the Badger state. She knew blizzards as well as the heat of August nights; she embraced the April showers and the almost violent beauty of crimson autumn days. These seasons fill the senses with sights and sounds, smells and tastes that found incarnation in her poetic verse. Analogies from nature permeated her poems.

In the dialogue of the above poem, Jessica Powers notes that nature has its beauty and grandeur. But, beneath the rocks and the rivers, there resides Love without beginning or end, the Love that undergirds every cell of every being. It was Light that swept over all creation giving it existence; it is Love that sustains and guides it still. Nature was but another sacramental means for this poet to grow in her love and praise of God.

Key Words in Jessica Powers' Lexicon

Over the years each of us develops our own vocabulary which expresses who we are and what we stand for. To know the lexicon of a person is to know a great deal about that individual. Jessica Powers had many words stored in her mind and heart, words that symbolized her values, dreams, hopes, and attitudes. Several words occur time and time again in her poetry and discourse, thereby revealing to the reader the inner workings of her heart. Here are five words from Jessica's lexicon that tell us much about this poet.

Come (33, 37). The Carmelite sisters often pray the beautiful Latin hymn, "Veni, Creator Spiritus"—"Come, Creator Spirit." Not surprisingly this "Veni," this "Come," was central to Jessica Powers' prayer life and poetic vocation. To maintain that "Come is the love song of our race," as found in the following poem, is a powerful proposition. It is a cry for Presence, it is "our basic word of individual wooing."

But there is mutuality in this word. Just as we ask God to come into our lives so, too, God invites us to come and follow the divine path. In fact, Jesus' own lexicon contained the word "Come," that invitation to dwell in his heart and home. "Come" is synonymous with discipleship when it is lived. Given Jessica Powers' love for this word, it is not surprising that Advent was an important season in her spiritual life.

Come Is the Love Song

Come is the love song of our race and Come
our basic word of individual wooing.
It lifts audacious arms of lowliness
to majesty's most amiable undoing,
to Godhood fleshed and cradled and made least.
It whispers through closed doors a hurry, hurry
to Tierce and fiery feast.
The liturgy of Advent plucks its bud
from the green shrub of love's compendium:
O Wisdom, Adonai, Root of Jesse
and sign by which the mouths of kings are dumb,
O Key, O Orient, King and Cornerstone,
O our Emmanuel, come.
And Paschaltide prepares an upper room
where burns the fuller bloom.
Come is the small sweet-smelling crib we carve
from fir and bear across December frost.

It is the shaft of the flame-hungry Church
in Paschal spring, or the heart's javelin tossed
privately at the clouds to pierce them through
and drown one in the flood of some amazing
personal Pentecost.

(49)

Wilderness (3, 65, 185). In contrast to the verdant
meadow, filled with much "juice and joy," the starkness
and aridity of the wilderness cause a foreboding in the
human soul. This poet knew that any geography, appar-
ently unvisited by love, is essentially a wasteland. But
once the water of God's grace (love) comes to the desert,
everything begins to bloom. Associated with wilderness
are several other words: lost-ness *(7, 11)*, melancholy
(23), darkness *(1, 22)*, emptiness *(91)*, frailty *(14)*, si-
lence *(24, 109)*, wretchedness *(88)*, loneliness *(18, 73,
114, 156)*. Listen now to a rejoicing wilderness:

AND WILDERNESS REJOICES

Land that was desolate, impassable,
is forest now where secrets find their voices.
The desert is inhabited and blooms.
One with the meadow, wilderness rejoices.

Lebanon's glory is its green possession
and Carmel's beauty. Visited by love,
wastelands are pastures for the Lamb at midday,
and living solitudes to hold the Dove.

Never again will patriarch prefigure
or lean precursor walk or prophet call.
Here is fulfillment. One has come and given
the Spirit Who is flame and festival.

Sower and Sown are here.
The bright groves flourish
and burn toward islands in the utmost sea.
Time has become a wilderness of presence
which too is essence of its jubilee.

Earth keeps its seasons and its liturgy,
as should the soul. Oh, come, green summer, blur
these wastes and let my soul in song declare
Who came by flesh and Who by fire to her.

(7)

Love (143, 159, 165, 185). Jessica Powers knew that
she was "a citizen of love." For her, God's love was the
source and destiny of her life. Continuously she reflected

on and prayed for this grace, and struggled in realizing the gap between God's love for her and her response which, by comparison, was so small. One can almost hear her groan as she writes, "I love you, God, with a penny match of love…" ("This Paltry Love," 48). Though she dreamt of love's glorious heights, in reality there was only a "puny spark" and no roaring fire. But there is more optimism when the poet compares love to a Creeping Charlie: "love is a simple plant like a Creeping Charlie; / once it takes root its talent is to spread." ("My Heart Ran Forth," 45). But the focus on human effort finally yields to divine grace as Jessica Powers declares herself a citizen of love and God's ambassador:

THE LITTLE NATION

Having no gift of strategy or arms,
no secret weapon and no walled defense,
I shall become a citizen of love,
that little nation with the blood-stained sod
where even the slain have power, the only country
that sends forth an ambassador to God.

Renouncing self and crying out to evil
to end its wars, I seek a land that lies

all unprotected like a sleeping child;
nor is my journey reckless and unwise.
Who doubts that love has an effective weapon
may meet with a surprise.

(39)

Beauty (20, 175). A large measure of poetry's power
lies in its relationship to beauty. While in no way dimin-
ishing truth and goodness, the poet has special claim to
emphasizing the beauty which, in its full form, is glory.
Jessica Powers was intrigued by light and glory, by the
beautiful. Her love for the beauty of nature and all of
creation, for trees, birds, and flowers, gave her much de-
light. But so did the internal beauty of a committed life,
of personal integrity, and of shared community. When a
soul is properly disposed, it surrenders and yields to the
grace of God's beauty, to the mystery of God's tremen-
dous love. (See also "Without Beauty," 97.)

BEAUTY, TOO, SEEKS SURRENDER

Love writes surrender as its due;
but how is beauty actor?
The heart remembers wound and loss
while mind sings benefactor.

God takes by love what yields to love,
then pours a glowing allness
past the demolished walls and towers
into the spirit's smallness.

God's beauty, too, surrender seeks
and takes in the will's lull
whatever lets itself be changed
into the beautiful.

And so, Michelangelo
has marked it out to be,
since beauty is the purging of
all superfluity.

The yielded soul that lifts its gaze
to harms past nature's claim
expects to have experience
of blade and file and flame.

(72)

Humility (117, 144, 178). The soul's response to an awareness of forgiveness and mercy is humility. Jessica Powers speaks of "the rich booty of humility" as she ponders the grace of divine forgiveness in her life. Humility flows, too, from a sense of one's total dependence on God, on the fact that all is gift and we can claim nothing, in the ultimate sense, as coming from us. Arrogance and pride are difficult to find in a poet who is constantly aware of "her inch of worth" (cf. "One Answer," 107).

There is a certain anonymity associated with humility, almost an embarrassment in seeing one's name affixed to a piece of creativity, for is not God the source of all beauty, truth and goodness? Yet, even here, humility demands that one assume partial responsibility as co-creator, however small, in God's plan of sharing life, love, and light.

HUMILITY

Humility is to be still
under the weathers of God's will.

It is to have no hurt surprise
when morning's ruddy promise dies,

when wind and drought destroy, or sweet
spring rains apostatize in sleet,

or when the mind and mouth remark
a superfluity of dark.

It is to have no troubled care
for human weathers anywhere.

And yet it is to take the good
with the warm hands of gratitude.

Humility is to have place
deep in the secret of God's face

where one can know, past all surmise,
that God's great will alone is wise,

where one is loved, where one can trust
a strength not circumscribed by dust.

It is to have a place to hide
when all is hurricane outside.

(92)

Another Wisconsin poet, Father Gordon Gilsdorf, speaks about God's lexicon:

I searched
God's lexicon
To fathom "Bethlehem"
And "Calvary." It simply said:
See "Love."

(Cf. "Lyrics for the Christian")[2]

Perhaps in the end, Jessica Power's lexicon was identical. Love is the Word, for God *is* love. Important as words were for Jessica Powers, it was the Reality behind the words that she sought—and, hopefully, now knows in its fullness.

CHAPTER 3

Selected Poems
Praying with Jessica Powers

P rayer is both unique and universal. Individuals and communities have their specific way of praying based on culture and traditions. Yet the underlying structure of prayer remains the same: the rhythm of listening and responding. As Hans Urs von Balthasar reminds us: "Prayer, as we can now see, is communication, in which God's word has the initiative, and we, at first, are simply listeners."[1]

Jessica Powers was a pray-er. She lived forty-seven years as a cloistered religious, spending many hours each day in prayer. She wrote out of her experience of encountering God in liturgical and personal prayer, in community, and in her experience of life. We, as beneficiaries, have access to some of her insights and encounters with the Lord. By reflectively meditating on her verse, we have an opportunity of encountering the Lord in our own unique way.

How to Begin

Take a period of no less than 20 minutes and begin by slowly reading the poem suggested. If possible, read it out loud and several times. Watch for images and metaphors that speak to your heart. Note any call to action that the Lord offers you. The goal is union with the Lord and a drawing forth into a life of fuller love and responsibility. If the poem speaks to you, there is no need to move on to the commentary and suggested prayer, but they are provided as an additional help.

Ten themes for prayer have been chosen, each followed by several suggested prayer periods. Since *freedom* is such a treasured value in our society, it is well to look at this gift from a spiritual point of view, for true freedom arises from a virtuous life. *Mercy,* another great gift from God, is the source of confidence and trust. God, who is rich in mercy, invites us to clutch his holy garments. *Spirituality,* according to our poetic guide, is about listening and loving. We live in God's Spirit to the extent that we are listeners and lovers.

Poets speak of life and *death.* For Jessica Powers, death is seen as a homecoming, one filled with surprise and delight. A fifth theme for prayer is *God's will.* What is the Lord asking us to do and how do we come to sing God's loving song? *Providence* is one of the most complex theological issues. Are we under regard? Does God care? What about evil? One of the most significant expressions of God's providential love is the gift of the *Eucharist*. Divine bread has been given to feed the hungers of the soul.

The last three themes are *the person of Jesus, simplicity* and *community*. Christian prayer centers on the *person of the Lord*. The question, "Who do you say the Son of Man is?" (Mt 16:13), still must be answered. Jesus calls us to lives of *simplicity*, that we might know the one thing necessary; no easy task in a world of great complexity. And, finally, it is in *community* that we experience God in a unique way. As members of the body of Christ, we are responsible for one another.

Saint Paul reminds us time and time again that, in our weakness, the Holy Spirit prays within us. Sometimes that Holy Spirit is sent through angels and poets. Jessica Powers, whose religious name was Sister Miriam of the Holy Spirit, by exercising her gift of poetry, has been a channel of God's Spirit of wisdom, joy, and love for many.

Prayer Period 1

Freedom

One of the greatest values of democracy is that of freedom. Often this refers to political and economic freedom. But there is another freedom as well: spiritual freedom.

How free are we to hear and respond to God's call? Do we truly possess this "deep" freedom which ultimately determines our destiny?

THE HOUSE AT REST

> *On a dark night*
> *Kindled in love with yearnings—*
> *Oh, happy chance!—*
>
> *I went forth unobserved,*
> *My house being now at rest.*

Saint John of the Cross

How does one hush one's house,
each proud possessive wall, each sighing rafter,
the rooms made restless with
remembered laughter
or wounding echoes, the permissive doors,
the stairs that vacillate from up to down,
windows that bring in color and event
from countryside or town,
oppressive ceilings and complaining floors?

The house must first of all accept the night.
Let it erase the walls and their display,

impoverish the rooms till they are filled
with humble silences; let clocks be stilled
and all the selfish urgencies of day.

Midnight is not the time to greet a guest.
Caution the doors against both foes and friends,
and try to make the windows understand
their unimportance when the daylight ends.
Persuade the stairs to patience, and deny
the passages their aimless to and fro.
Virtue it is that puts a house at rest.
How well repaid that tenant is, how blest
who, when the call is heard,
is free to take his kindled heart and go.

(122)

Hushing

Poets ask good questions—William Blake: "Did he [God] smile his work to see, / Did he who made the lamb make thee [the tiger]?" Gerard Manley Hopkins: "What is so beautiful as spring?" And Jessica Powers: "How does one hush one's house?" How do we quiet our frenetic minds and troubled hearts? To answer that question, one would think, would be the province only of the wise.

73

What are the factors that create inner turmoil? Their numbers are legion: walls that display diplomas and trophies, shelves upon shelves of books and knick-knacks, banners with their one-liners. Then there are the rafters that carry not only the heavy weight of the roof, but also the weight of unrequited love and lost friendship. Add to this room upon room of parties and gala celebrations, room upon room of hurt and bitter tears.

Even the stairs of our houses are ambivalent, not clear about ascending into the future with hope or descending into the past with its ambiguous successes and crushing failures. The windows, so numerous and reaching out in every direction, inundate us with millions of events and thousands of colors. Our senses are overwhelmed. To compound matters we must deal with oppression and complaints pressing in upon us from outside and within, leaving us weary and distraught.

Hushing is a noble art. It is that grace and discipline by which we quiet the soul and draw it beyond the multiplicity of events and the immediacy of a thousand voices into a center, a still point, where the one thing necessary is found: peace—that peace willed by God, the gift of the Holy Spirit.

Gracious God, teach us how to hush our houses so that we might live deeply. Send your Spirit to still the incessant voices and events that plague our fatigued souls. Hush our houses. Grant us the order and peace which only you can give.

Lessons

The acceptance of darkness, of not knowing, is a difficult task. We yearn for light and certitude, we fear ignorance and the lack of control that it brings. Saying "yes" to the dark is a courageous, risky act, but a necessary one if we are to encounter the mystery of God. Mary, in the Annunciation mystery, uttered her "fiat" while still not knowing how the request made of her was to be fulfilled.

For the "hush" to come, we must also forget, however temporarily, all the displays that line our walls and are essentially self-referential: *our* degrees, *our* matted photographs of friendships, *our* trophies of elks and economic gains, *our* prize calligraphy of a Shakespearean sonnet. Now, in the night of prayer, all is erased and forgotten. As we empty our memory and imagination of their contents we fill the inner space with a silence at once humble and holy. The soul is preparing for yet another divine advent. We slip from time, with the clock's incessant ticking into the eternal Now. We let go of all the emergencies and the urgencies that are so often directed to the fulfillment of our needs.

We enter here the land of detachment, *kenosis*, letting go. Part of the spiritual triad supporting our relationship with God is asceticism (prayer and service being the other two legs). This mortification is a willingness not to cling to things. Freedom is the goal of this graced discipline, a freedom opening us to love and to fullness of life. This discipline is most difficult in a culture insisting that having (consumerism and materialism) is the root of happiness. To go empty, to live in waiting, to refuse a life of acquisitiveness is to take the narrow path, the less traveled road.

> *Lord Jesus, you emptied yourself of your divinity in taking on the confines of our human condition. Help us to follow your way, the way of obedience and self-giving. Free us from all that holds us in bondage. Send your Spirit of joyful detachment into our hearts.*

The Call

Before the call is heard, more work must be done in hushing our house. Certainly the Christian way of life calls us to hospitality. We are to welcome friend and foreigner, family and foe. But the time comes in each of our lives (call it midnight or the hour before dawn) when solitude and silence are demanded. The other hours of the day are sufficient to address the needs of the poor and the hurting.

Doors are to be heeded lest, being open too long, a draft chills the soul unto death. As for the windows, they too lack significance when dark descends. Even being open to too much moonlight renders a disservice to the soul yearning for God. Impatient stairs need conversion and well-earned rest. And the passages, our aimless hallways directing traffic now right, now left, need to be denied their claim to ceaseless activity.

So what is it that ultimately hushes our house? Virtue! Herein lies rest for the soul and the peace that is beyond all understanding. It is living in conformity to God's will. It is the way of obedience. The tenant of this rented house is well compensated with happiness because he or she, now dwelling in a hushed house, will discern God's intimate calling. More, because of the virtue of obedience, that tenant will say yes to the divine commission—the mandate to bring Life-Love-Light into a broken world.

Loving God, you both call and gift us to be your people. We struggle to hear your voice, we resist your charge to be salt and light to the world. Grace us with solitude and obedience. Most of all, enkindle within us the fire of your Holy Spirit. In the end our hushed houses will welcome all who enter to join you at the one table.

Prayer Period 2

Mercy

Justice leads to peace. We are mandated by the Gospel to be people of justice, protecting and promoting the rights of all, especially those who are most vulnerable—the young and the old, the powerless... But, when we come face to face with God, we desire not justice but mercy. These are the garments we cling to as we seek God's gift of salvation.

THE GARMENTS OF GOD

God sits on a chair of darkness in my soul.
He is God alone, supreme in His majesty.
I sit at His feet, a child in the dark beside Him;
my joy is aware of His glance

and my sorrow is tempted
to nest on the thought that His face
is turned from me.
He is clothed in the robes of His mercy,
voluminous garments—
not velvet or silk and affable to the touch,
but fabric strong for a frantic hand to clutch,
and I hold to it fast with the fingers of my will.
Here is my cry of faith, my deep avowal
to the Divinity that I am dust.
Here is the loud profession of my trust.
I need not go abroad
to the hills of speech or the hinterlands of music
for a crier to walk in my soul where all is still.
I have this potent prayer through good or ill:
here in the dark I clutch the garments of God.

(21)

Divine Indwelling

Early on in our religious training, many of us heard
that we are temples of the Holy Spirit. This is one of Saint
Paul's central doctrines: God's Spirit has taken up resi-
dence in our souls. The divine indwelling is a matter of

faith, the belief that God is present in the darkness of our souls filling them with light and warmth. We might not "feel" God sitting there, though there may be signs of that presence in our works of justice, words of affirmation, moments of spontaneous prayer. We do well to sit, like Mary, at the Lord's feet to await God's word.

In the silence and darkness our awareness can turn in one of two directions. With the eyes of joy we are conscious that we are being looked at with love. How could it be otherwise since God is a God of love? John of the Cross confirms our confidence by stating that "when God looks, [God] loves and grants favors."[2]

There is, however, another option which comes to us in the form of a temptation. Could God turn away from us? What if the prodigal son's father did not await the son's return but, rather, in anger and disgust disinherited his very son who squandered his inheritance? Our sorrow and guilt and shame, like a weary bird, is drawn to rest on the possibility that God has rejected us because of our sin and weakness.

Prodigal God, you dwell deep within us through the gift of your Spirit. In childlike humility, let us experience your loving glance and forever banish the thought that you have turned away from us in judgment and anger. Give us joy; take away our sorrow. Never let us be parted from you.

Rich in Mercy

God's lexicon is small, containing only such words as love, compassion, and forgiveness. God's wardrobe is limited as well, consisting primarily of mercy. Indeed, God is *"dives in misericordia"*—rich in mercy. We are the beneficiaries of this garment. Aware of our sin and guilt, we come before God in need, not seeking justice but only divine mercy. King David heard the words of Nathan the prophet: "You are the man!" (2 Sm 12:7). You are the man guilty of deception, adultery, murder. David, in deep humility, confessed his sins and reached out for the mercy and not the justice of God.

This mercy, made manifest in the cross, is anything but a gentle fabric. It's burlap. It's coarse. It's made with wood and the blood of the Lamb. No velvet or softness here, but material of substance and endurance. It will never wear out, for it is created out of love which, in the face of sin, we call mercy.

Like David, we must make a decision. The sinful king, by an honest act of the will, reached out in pain and sought the garment of God. A king is not supposed to have a frantic hand, a frightened heart. But then, a king is not supposed to violate his people. So, with the "fingers of his will," David grasped God's mercy, was forgiven, and then was given another son as a consolation.

God of mercy, robed in compassion and love, may we trust always in your forgiving ways. You are rich in mercy and extravagant in your kindness. Empower us to hold fast in faith to your robes of grace. Grant us the peace of reconciliation.

Cry of Faith

David's faith was more than a matter of words. He fasted, prayed, and mourned. His faith was grounded in the historical knowledge of God's love, going all the way back to the time he was called as a youth to be God's anointed. We, too, have been called by name; we, too, have been commissioned. In the very midst of darkness and sin, we are capable of uttering our silent cry of faith by clinging to God's voluminous garments.

Our confession is one of humility. We are dust. We are radically indigent. Yet, we are totally gifted and sustained at every moment by God's indwelling Spirit. Confession here is not just of sin, but of faith in a providential God.

Trust is the grace needed and sought. Our reaching

out for the robes of mercy is a mighty profession. We cannot claim "self-reliance." Such a profession would leave us in utter despair. Rather, we rely on the help of God and the promise of divine presence. To profess our confidence by holding on to the hem of God's garments is a powerful witness to the working of grace.

Give us, Lord, give us faith, trust, and confidence. In the dark world of doubt and distrust, we flounder and become disoriented. Draw us within reach of your mercy and, in the depth of our humanity, enable us to profess our utter dependence upon you.

Potent Prayer

Speech and music are fitting ways to praise and thank God for the gift of divine mercy. Gathering for a penance service, the community, in song and petition, expresses its faith and rejoices in the healing sacrament. At times, however, in the solitude and silence of the soul, neither word nor melody seem appropriate. Thus, there are many ways to thank God for divine gifts, many ways to be united to our loving, merciful God.

Prayer is powerful. Whether in times of prosperity or trial, we are called to lift up our minds and hearts to the Lord. In adoration our prayer focuses on God's very being, in thanksgiving on God's gifts, in petition on our need for God's help—powerful, potent prayers one and all.

But there is yet another prayer: seeking forgiveness. Deep in the darkness of our souls, alongside God's chair, we humbly cling to the robes of God's voluminous garments of mercy. What a potent, wordless prayer this silent clinging is; what a powerful, stirring act of faith; what stupendous trust!

Gracious God, teach us how to pray in word, in song, in silence. Instruct us in the ways of faith and trust. Our sins are before us always. May we cling to your garments of love and mercy and thereby experience your peace. May we teach each other this fine art of clinging, and help one another to know your mercy and peace.

Prayer Period 3

Spirituality

Every person has a spiritual life. How well it is tended and nurtured is another matter. Spirituality embraces all of life, but when we come down to the essentials, two qualities of spiritual living stand out: living with the Spirit

of God in listening and loving, and then being attentive
and responding to what the Lord asks of us.

To Live with the Spirit

To live with the Spirit of God is to be a listener.
It is to keep the vigil of mystery, earthless and still.
One leans to catch the stirring of the Spirit,
strange as the wind's will.

The soul that walks where the wind of the
Spirit blows
turns like a wandering weather vane toward love.
It may lament like Job or Jeremiah,
echo the wounded hart, the mateless dove.
It may rejoice in spaciousness of meadow
that emulates the freedom of the sky.
Always it walks in waylessness, unknowing;
it has cast down forever from its hand
the compass of the whither and the why.

To live with the Spirit of God is to be a lover.
It is becoming love, and like to Him
toward Whom we strain with metaphors
of creatures:
fire-sweep and water-rush and the wind's whim.

The soul is all activity, all silence;
and though it surges Godward to its goal,
it holds, as moving earth holds sleeping noonday,
the peace that is the listening of the soul.

(38)

Listening

Spirituality is an illusive term; even more so, our futile attempts to "comprehend" the Holy Spirit. Our finite minds and hearts stumble as we walk in the land of mystery.

Perhaps living a spiritual life, living in the Holy Spirit, is easier than we imagine. Maybe all we have to do, in grace, is to listen and to love. To be a listener (and a see-er) is to be present to the great mystery of life. Keeping watch at dawn—as a chrysalis opens, as a child is born, as a friend is dying—is to be plunged into the realm of the spiritual.

Within those moments and events, the Spirit of God is astir as Life-Love-Light. We lean, we stand on tiptoe, to discern these times of grace. Like the strange ways of the wind, God's grace comes from all quarters, unexpected, filled with power, surprising even the most alert.

We also listen, with a discerning heart, to those forces that are anti-mystery, anti-Love-Life-Light. These are other spirits that seek to attract our time and energy—and from which we must flee—for not all winds blow us home.

> *Spirit of the living God, give us good ears, discerning eyes, sensitive touch. Help us recognize your advents, and grace us to respond with joy and courage. May we live in your presence forever.*

Trusting God's Providence

Weather vanes appear fickle in their apparent directionlessness. But not the Spirit-filled weather vane that yields only to divine breezes, zephyrs of grace. So, too, the people that walk the road of discipleship. That walk embraces all seasons, times of lamentation, and profound loneliness. Walking with God has its ecstatic moments like those of a lamb frolicking in an open meadow or the windhover freely circling the vastness of the sky.

Sorrow or joy, ultimately, are not at issue for the soul walking the Spirit's way. What matters is surrender to "God's undivided sway," a yielding to God's will which no map or compass reveal. Trust empowers us to walk in waylessness, down the path of unknowing. Living with questions and not demanding answers is an experience of trusting in God's providential ways.

Spirit of fire and wind, help us to walk in your way. Fill us with trust and faith, relying not on human certitude, but on your gracious will. Be present in all our sorrow and joys that we may not falter. Blow where you will and bring us home.

Vocation of Love

Authentic listening leads to sacrificial loving. God is Love and we, made to the image of God, are born to receive, bear, and share that love. Love contains the energy of fire, water, and wind. Love is a lifelong process of even greater care, reverence, and generosity. Our whole being strains to attain our mission of being joyful conduits of God's love, light, and life.

In the striving we, at times, plunge into active ministry as we visit the sick and imprisoned, welcome the alien and exiled, instruct the young and comfort the old. Then we again withdraw into solitude to be alone with our loving God, seeking in contemplation the immediacy of the divine gaze. Our main task is to surge, ascend, climb toward God—a God who alone can satisfy our hunger for the infinite. Restless, we are yet hopeful that one day we will be possessed by God's tender embrace.

In all of this there is a peace, a listening, a loving which quiets our striving hearts. Though everything is in motion, there is a still point, a center of rich tranquillity. If our listening and loving are deep, no demands or exterior responsibilities can shatter that inner assurance of God's presence, our peace. Our commission is to live in and out of Presence, experiencing its joy in word and deed.

Come, Holy Spirit, come. Make us grow in love so that you might be known and adored. Transform our minds and hearts and let Jesus live in our innermost being. Only then shall we truly be listeners and lovers, your beloved daughters and sons.

Prayer Period 4
Death

Back in 1975, Ernst Becker wrote *The Denial of Death* in which he describes the modern world's approach to death's great mystery. As indicated, the typical response is one of denial, avoidance, cover-up. Lacking a vision of the beyond and of heaven, there are few choices to what seems to be death's finality. Faith does provide an alternative. Death, in its last breath, is a homecoming.

The spirit, newly freed from earth,
is all amazed at the surprise
of her belonging: suddenly
as native to eternity
to see herself, to realize
the heritage that lets her be
at home where all this glory lies.

By naught foretold could she have guessed
such welcome home: the robe, the ring,
music and endless banqueting,
these people hers; this place of rest
known, as of long remembering
herself a child of God and pressed
with warm endearments to His breast.

(53)

Faith's Vast Heritage

Christian faith holds that we come from God, we live
in God, and one day we are destined to return home to
God. Death marks that homecoming where we experi-
ence a freedom from all the restraints of time and space

as we are drawn into eternity. It takes us by surprise, this belonging to things eternal, this transcending of our earthly geography. We were indeed in exile, in the shadowlands, and now, passing through the portal of death, we are given a gracious, homey welcome.

A new vision emerges. We are native to eternity, drawn into the mystery of God. Time now proves foreign and our own nation a place of exile. Death opens the soul to the Divine. Dwelling in God's presence, the presence of Love-Light-Life, we taste the Beatific Vision where it is no longer a matter of faith since we are now in the very presence of the Triune God.

Glory and beauty await the freed soul. A vast heritage containing one's signature causes deep joy. Only on the other side of death could the soul endure so much light and radiance. What joy to be surrounded by the fullness of Love and to experience it as entirely natural to our deepest self.

Lord Jesus, because of your suffering, death, and resurrection, you have conquered sin and death. Now we have a way back home into your glory. The cross has set us free and fills our souls with your glory. Send your Spirit to help us so to live as to die in your love.

The Welcome

Few could have predicted the welcome home given to the prodigal son by his extravagant father. Out came the robe, then the ring for his finger, and more, the joy of music and dance and banqueting far into the night. The only sour note rose out of the heart of the elder son who was incapable of understanding and accepting his father's mercy. Bitterness clouded joy when such unlimited compassion was interpreted as an act of injustice.

The spirit, freed from earth through death, is given a similar welcome home. More important than the garb and the meal is the solidarity felt with the communion of saints. This is the community to which one truly belongs, those souls who walked the gospel path of love, compassion, and forgiveness. Deeper than one's ties to a genetic family is this community of like-minded and like-hearted souls. What joy to know such communion!

Two wonderful graces fill the souls in this place of rest we call heaven. One is the certitude that we are truly children of God. Our identity is confirmed and we finally are convinced about "whose we are." Second, the grace of intimacy is known through the expression of being drawn deeply into the heart of God—"pressed with warm endearments to His breast." All loneliness and any sense of alienation are gone. We are one with God and with one another. What a homecoming!

> Gracious God, your mercy knows no limits. Your heart rejoices upon our return home. Every grace of hospitality is given to us though undeserving. Give us a vision of this place of rest, this heaven where all those who followed the way of Jesus now dwell. May we know the tenderness of your embrace and see the radiance of your glory.

Prayer Period 5
God's Will

In the great prayer of the Church we ask that God's kingdom come, that God's will be done. Herein lies the mission and ministry of Jesus. As stated in John's Gospel, Jesus came that "all may have life and have it to the full" (Jn 10:10). Doing God's will rather than our own is one of the constant tensions that all pilgrims face.

THE WILL OF GOD

> Time has one song alone. If you are heedful
> and concentrate on sound with all your soul,

you may hear the song
of the beautiful will of God,
soft notes or deep sonorous tones that roll
like thunder over time.
Not many have the hearing for this music,
and fewer still have sought it as sublime.

Listen, and tell your grief: But God is singing!
God sings through all creation with His will.
Save the negation of sin, all is His music,
even the notes that set their roots in ill
to flower in pity, pardon or sweet humbling.
Evil finds harshness of the rack and rod
in tunes where good finds tenderness and glory.

The saints who loved have died of this pure music,
and no one enters heaven till he learns,
deep in his soul at least, to sing with God.

(19)

God's Will

In our noisy world it is difficult to listen to one an-
other. How much more difficult to attune our ears to hear
the silent music of God's will which fills every minute of

every day. Here is the song of songs, the melody of God's will which finds expression in the prophet Micah who states that God requires only that we act justly, love tenderly, walk humbly in faith (cf. Mi 6:8). But to hear this song demands an intense concentration. How many truly hear this song? How many seek it as the most sublime grace possible? Not many, suggests the poet.

The notes and tones of this divine hymn are sometimes soft, sometimes sonorous. In times of personal sorrow or national anguish this song will be a lamentation. When love is celebrated and peace is fostered then we hear alleluia and a blare of trumpets. Perhaps our primary vocation is to be glad instruments of this symphony which, when it is heard by others, will enable them to experience the beautiful will of God.

As we pray the great prayer "Our Father," the phrase "your will be done" must not be spoken or sung lightly. As C. S. Lewis reminds us, there are only two kinds of people—those who do God's will and those who do their own.[3] Seeking God's will over our own, presupposes a radical conversion. It is the work of the Holy Spirit that transforms our minds and hearts so that they center, not on our own agenda, but on God's kingdom, a kingdom of peace, truth, charity, freedom, and justice.

*Lord God, at this very moment you sing your love song to our
fragile, broken, deaf world. Help us to hear the harmony of
your will, help us to see the beauty of your divine plan. Gifted
with courage we will seek your music and enter your dance.*

God: The Divine Songster

Our sorrow and grief tell us that God is absent, gone,
nowhere to be found. Our faith, informed by graced lis-
tening, has good news. God is now singing all over cre-
ation a composition that fills us with joy and drives out
all sadness. Of course, it is the song of love, God's tender,
abiding, redeeming love made visible in Jesus through
the working of the Spirit. It is a Trinitarian hymn that
can be heard in the mysteries of creation, redemption,
and sanctification.

Only one thing is not of God's will: the fact and mys-
tery of sin. Only this disobedience, this "missing the
mark," this breaking the web of relationships, is foreign
to the will of God. Other notes, although not sinful in
nature, are indeed heavy in their suffering. These do find
a place in the divine composition. These somber phrases,
distasteful to our weak human nature, eventually can bear
much fruit if integrated into our spiritual life. Three spe-

cific blessings can emerge from such integration: pity, pardoning, and humbling. Each of these conforms us more closely to the person of Jesus, the One who knew the power of mercy, forgiveness, and poverty of spirit.

On this pilgrim journey we must interpret the songs that accompany us. If our eyes and ears are infected with evil, God's will takes on the appearance of anger and harshness. Painful images fill our imagination. But for those who hear only goodness in the melody of God's will, the journey will be filled with glory and rich tenderness. The tune is the same; the hearing depends on who we are deep within.

Come, Holy Spirit, come. Open our ears to the sound of your voice, open our eyes to the mystery of creation. May the negation of sin be far from our experience. May we turn from evil and all its harshness and come to know the tenderness and glory that dwell in the hearts of all those who hear and heed God's singing.

Entering Heaven

Saints die in various ways: John the Baptist was beheaded as was Saint Thomas More; Saint Thérèse of Lisieux died of tuberculosis at the age of 24; Saint

Maximilian Kolbe was executed by the Nazis after volunteering to take the place of a man sentenced to die. What empowered these individuals, and millions of others, to die for their faith? They all were given the grace of love; they all died surrounded by the pure music of God's love for the world.

Ultimately there is only one gate into the divine presence. It is not the door of merit or personal effort. It is not the portal of success and surmised innocence. Rather, the door of heaven opens to those who have learned, not just the theology of God's will, but who have participated in singing with God the divine melody of love. Even those who cannot carry a tune know heaven, because their singing is contained in their deeds of justice, sacrifice, and self-giving.

All this singing goes on deep in the soul, deep in the center of our true selves. From this rich interiority there emerge both small and great acts of kindness, tiny and large deeds of compassion, comforting and challenging words of love. Just as we never walk alone, having been promised the grace of God's presence, so, too, we never sing alone. The Holy Spirit sings within us the heavenly song of the divine will. To live in harmony with this melody is to know peace.

We are called to be saints, Lord. Only if you gift us with the
"perfection of charity" can we measure up to the holiness you
desire that we live. Plant your song of love in us. Send your
Spirit to chant that melody night and day. May we know now
the beauty of your voice.

Prayer Period 6

Providence

Does God provide for us? Are our prayers heard and
responded to? What about the problem of evil and all
the innocent who are destroyed without rhyme or rea-
son? These are questions that philosophers and scholars
have wrestled with throughout the centuries. Poets, too,
have their response, the following one is made in faith.

THE CEDAR TREE

In the beginning, in the unbeginning
of endlessness and of eternity,
God saw this tree.
He saw these cedar branches bending low
under the full exhaustion of the snow.
And since he set no wind of day to rising,
this burden of beauty and this burden of cold,

(whether the wood breaks or the branches hold)
must be of His devising.

There is a cedar similarly decked
deep in the winter of my intellect
under the snow, the snow,
the scales of light its limitations tell.

I clasp this thought: from all eternity
God who is good looked down upon this tree
white in the weighted air,
and of another cedar reckoned well.
He knew how much each tree,
each twig could bear.
He counted every snowflake as it fell.

(176)

Divine Providence

Modern physics attempts to chart the beginning of
things; millions, billions of years ago it all began, scien-
tists assert. Astronomy tells us that our planet earth is
situated in a relatively small galaxy in a vast field of count-
less other galaxies, whirling through space thousands of
miles per hour. Our minds and our imaginations stagger

before such horizons of time and space. We lack a proper perspective to comprehend it all.

Simple faith cuts through scientific conjectures and asserts in dark confidence that God created it all by way of divine providence. God saw this tree in this particular cedar swamp. This nation, this triumph, this failure of history, and this beat of my human heart are all embraced in God's foreknowledge. Nothing goes unnoticed.

Simple faith does not necessarily exclude tough questions. When cedar branches bear the beauty and burden of snow and cold, there is a good chance that they will break and, severed from the tree, they will die. A rising wind would free the branch from its weight and preserve its life. More snowfall would surely end it all. Where is this God's loving providence? Where in this is God's devising?

God of providence and love, enlighten our minds and hearts to understand the workings of your will. So often we see trees fallen by winter storms and hurricanes; so often we see nations destroying nations. Our faith is shaken in such moments. We ask: "Could this be of your devising?" We stumble once again before the mystery of death, the enigma of evil.

Human Interiority

Just as nature is often weighted with burdens, be they snow or storms, so, too, the human mind and heart find themselves under extreme pressures rising from psychological or spiritual stress. From our personal experience and that of those around us, it is obvious that there are breaking points. The news of a suicide comes in a too-early phone call. We visit acquaintances in the psychiatric ward. Books abound which encourage people to continue their medication in order to balance the delicate chemical composition of the brain.

When winter comes to our intellect or heart and we find these faculties under the snow, we feel once again the great limitations of life. Sometimes great weights can be borne; at other times even a slight snowfall hints at collapse. Life is precarious.

Lord of compassion and love, you know the limits of our spirit. We are finite creatures, limited in the burdens we bear. Send your Spirit to give us strength and knowledge. And when we are weighted by worries and hardships, ease our burden and grant us your peace.

Profound Confidence

Faith is about trust and confidence. It is about a radical assurance that God's love surrounds, sustains, and guides us still. Saint Paul had this faith even in the midst of trials and his execution by the sword. As the final snowflake fell that severed Saint Paul from this life, he trusted that his mission had been accomplished and that it was time to return to the Lord. He spoke eloquently in claiming that the burdens and trials of this life cannot be compared with the glory to come (cf. Rom 8:17).

It is well to clasp the faith-filled thought that God gazes upon us at every moment with love. God knows the anguish and pain that each of us carries. He knows how much each of us can bear. Hanging onto this belief opens us to experience the grace that we are not alone. Even in the darkest of nights, the divine Light is with us. Even if the weight of trials must be endured, the thought of a providential Presence offers the reassurance of being accompanied as we bear our cross.

As Jesus bore the weight of the cross, and ultimately his crucifixion, one might imagine his Father counting the lashes, the thorns in the crown, the drops of his blood. But this was not the counting of a bookkeeper. Rather, it was that of a compassionate Father whose eyes were filled with tears. Sacrificial love runs in the family. The weight on Calvary was felt in heaven.

Deepen our faith, Lord, in your gracious providence. You journey with us in sunshine and in rain. You carry so much of our burden that we might one day exclaim: our yoke is easy and our burden is light. It is your Spirit that empowers us to be the cedar tree you wish us to be.

Prayer Period 7

Eucharist

The Eucharist is so many things: a sacrament of love, a sign of unity, a memorial of Jesus' death and resurrection, the summit and source of the Christian life… And the Eucharist does so many things: completes Christian initiation, anticipates eternal life, makes us sharers in the Body and Blood of Christ, commits us to serve the poor… So it is well that we take a poetic trip back to a moment when Jesus took, blessed, and gave thanks over some small barley loaves.

THE LEFTOVERS

With twenty loaves of bread Elisha fed
the one hundred till they were satisfied,

and Scripture tells us there was bread left over.
Jesus did more: with five small barley loaves
and two dried fish he fed five thousand men,
together with their wives and children, all
neatly arranged upon the cushioned grass.
The awed disciples, when the crowd had eaten,
gathered up what was left: twelve baskets full.

Who then received these fragments? Hopefully,
the least (though not less favored) and the poor.
I think of those who always seem to get
the leavings from the banqueting of others,
the scraps of bread, of life, that goodness saves.
I pray that they come proudly when invited,
make merry at their meal, and have their fill,
and rise up thankfully, remembering
the fragments, too, were miracles of love.

(112)

A Hungry World

The hungers of the heart are many: the hunger for
meaning, for depth, for wholeness, for love, for bread.
When these hungers are not met, people get sick and
die. Elisha knew this, as did Jesus. Their mission in life

was to reach out to those in need and to assist them in their deepest hungers. Although here the focus is on food—loaves and fishes—we know that both prophets had deeper designs in mind.

The disciples were awed at the workings of Jesus. Always there were leftovers. No matter how much Jesus gave of himself, there was still more time, energy, and care to be had. Twelve baskets of loaves and fishes are merely symbols of the extravagance and bounty of God's self-giving.

Bountiful God, may we emulate you in your generosity. We have been given so much, others are in such need. Help us to realize that the more we give the more we will be given so that that bounty may also be shared. Always there will be leftovers if only our hearts are generous.

Miracles of Love

Does God have a preferential option for the least and the poor? Are these the ones who are to be given the leftovers from the banquets of those who have? God's love is universal and shows no partiality. Yet, those in greatest need deserve our urgent attention; hopefully, we will not share leavings and scraps with them, but the very best we have. Before the banquet even begins, stewardship should be exercised in sharing "off the top," what has been given to us. The miracle may well have been not only the multiplication of the loaves, but the decision of some of the crowd to share what they had with those thousands who had nothing.

All are invited to the banquet of life. All are encouraged to come proudly and thankfully to the Eucharistic meal set before humankind. Jesus himself is the miracle of love who becomes bread that is broken. He came to save sinners and those who were lost in darkness. He came to embrace the prodigal and the outcast, for they, too, are part of God's family. Perhaps in the end there will be no leftovers. All will have their fill and know the satiation of their deepest hunger for intimacy with God.

And then, having been filled, we become a Eucharistic people by being for others what Jesus has been for us. And, as we leave the banquet hall, we read an implicit sign above the door: "You are now entering the mission field."

It is in the Eucharist, Lord, that we experience the miracle of love in its fullness. You have shared with us, the rich and the poor, the saint and the sinner, your body and blood. Empower us to be eucharist to one another. Make us a generous people.

Help us perpetuate the miracle of love by being a caring and loving community.

Prayer Period 8
The Person of Jesus

The gospel question: "Who do you say that I am?" must be answered by each of us. Who is this historical Jesus, this risen Christ? As disciples, we each must invoke the Holy Spirit to open our hearts to the revelation of Jesus. Peter proclaimed Jesus to be the Messiah, not by any great personal insight, but because the Father graced Peter with divine revelation. That same grace is available to us.

CHRIST IS MY UTMOST NEED

Late, late the mind confessed:
wisdom has not sufficed.
I cannot take one step into the light
without the Christ.

Late, late the heart affirmed:
wild do my heart beats run
when in the blood stream sings one wish away
from the Incarnate Son.

Christ is my utmost need.
I lift each breath, each beat for Him to bless,
knowing our language cannot overspeak
our frightening helplessness.

Here where proud morning walks
and we hang wreaths on power and
self-command,
I cling with all my strength unto a nail-
investigated hand.

Christ is my only trust.
I am my fear since, down the lanes of ill,
my steps surprised a dark Iscariot
plotting in my own will.

Past nature called, I cry
who clutch at fingers and at tunic folds,
"Lay not on me, O Christ, this fastening.
Yours be the hand that holds."

(152)

Wisdom

Plato and Aristotle and great philosophers down
through the ages have offered us a tremendous body of

wisdom. Their insights into the world and human nature continue to sustain us. They were given gifts of great intellects and they used their gifts responsibly. We are indebted to them.

But human wisdom does not suffice. Though it leads us toward the light, only the person of Christ provides ultimate meaning, ultimate love. The mind makes its confession and resolves to see Christ at the center of the universe.

Lord Jesus, you are the Way, the Truth, and the Life. You are also our Light and the Wisdom and the Power of God. May we not be too late in confessing our insufficiency, or too late in turning to you that we might truly see life for what it is.

Affirmation

When the heart beats in wild patterns, no matter how late in life, we ought to affirm the presence of some special grace. But it is more than the gift of human friendship or health, more than success in ministry that we affirm. With our hearts we affirm the presence of the Incarnate Son, God-made-man.

Not only does the mind confess, but the heart affirms the love given to us in the person of Jesus. Both faculties falter in the face of such tremendous grace: that God would become one of us so that we might know, for certain, divine love and mercy. Hearts devoid of this knowledge or experience will always be restless and empty.

Create in us, O Lord, new hearts. Send your Spirit within us so that we might affirm your presence and respond to your voice. Cause our hearts to beat wildly; empower us to live your word with joy.

Helplessness

We are a needy people. Every breath is a gift; every heartbeat is the work of God. It is impossible to exaggerate our radical poverty and indebtedness to God. Gratitude should flood our souls as we ponder God's goodness to us. Every hour of every day we should bless and thank God for divine goodness.

We need food and shelter, friendship and support. Most of all we need Christ to show us the way and to empower us with his Spirit so that we may do the Father's will. Jesus is our utmost need, whether we feel it or not. The fulfillment of all other needs cannot satisfy the soul's deepest longings and desires. Only the person of Jesus can do that.

Though we are often frightened by our helplessness, yet we know that you are near, Lord. We trust in your presence and love for us. Fulfill our needs. Give us our daily bread, especially the Bread of eternal life which sustains us on the journey.

Temptations

There are many things that we can cling to in life: pleasures, persons, power, prestige, and possessions. We especially "crown" our freedom, covering it with flowers and tribute, as if it were our messiah. Pride in such things has a short life span. Yet, generation after generation we are deceived or deceive ourselves into believing that power and domination are what life is all about.

But, there is another response to our clinging and search for meaning: holding onto the hand of the crucified Christ with all one's strength and will. Although not a popular choice, the poet Jessica made this her choice. The Lord Jesus would be the object of her heart's desire. And, as Saint Paul expressed this ultimate choice for God, perhaps Jessica also found that nothing compared to sharing in the life, death, and resurrection of Jesus (cf. Phil 3:7–11).

Jesus crucified, help us to know the meaning of the cross and the love and mercy it symbolizes. May we cling to you and your way, not being deceived by values that cannot satisfy. Give us courage to cling to your very self.

Trust

The Psalmist cries out: "All my trust is in your promise." Indeed, all my trust is in the person of Christ. Some people rely on "horses and chariots," bank accounts and public recognition. Jesus is worthy of trust because he keeps his promise, a promise of Presence for all times.

However, trust does not eliminate all fear. We are weak creatures and are capable of experiencing extreme betrayal. Within each person there lives a "dark Iscariot," greedy, cowardly, self-seeking. Two lanes can be traveled: the lane of good or the lane of ill. Decisions made at this interior crossroad can determine our destiny.

Guide us, Lord, down the path of righteousness and justice. All our trust is in your promise of Presence and the gift of the Holy Spirit. Do not allow us to be parted from you. Do not let us be surprised by the Iscariot within.

Plea

Poetry as prayer. The poet cries out for God's gracious assistance. Perhaps one's past history reflects, all too well, a life not lived with Christ as its utmost need. Now all is different. One thing alone matters: union with Christ. Only the hand of Christ can hold us in peace and deep joy.

Once again the soul clings to Christ, clutches the tunic of God's love and the fingers of Christ's mercy. But the soul must be held, held by the graciousness of God, who forgives and blesses those who confess and have faith. And when the divine hand grasps our own, all will be well.

Hear the cry of our voice, O Lord, and come to our assistance. Grab hold of our wills and make them your own. As we reach out to you, embrace us in your love and empower us to do your will. Christ is our utmost and most precious need.

Prayer Period 9

Simplicity

In a complex world and culture, is it possible any longer to believe in simplicity? The multiplicity of relationships, the incessant call of duties and pleasures, the rapidity of change in a post-modern world, all place the simple life in the land of dreams and wishes. And yet, there may well be one thing necessary. Perhaps if we return to what is essential, putting first things first, we might again experience some joy, a modicum of peace.

RETURN

This was the fever that beset my years,
that led by pride, I put my aim too high.
I strained my spirit, grasping at the moon;
my heart I wearied, reaching for the sky.

My thoughts like ways and social climbers were
who spurned their childhood home for vistas dim.
I cast the little virtues from my hand
and wrote brief notes to stars and seraphim.

I must come home again to simple things:
robins and buttercups and bumblebees,
laugh with the elves and try again to find
a leprechaun behind the hawthorn trees.

(157)

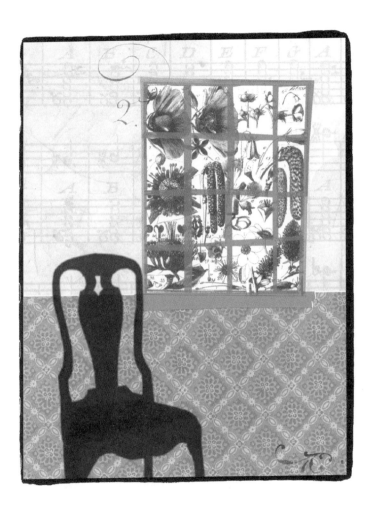

The Fever

There is a contagious fever that spreads rapidly throughout the human race; it goes by the name of ambition and pride. Our fragile egos seek to assert their importance by achievement: taking first prize in a literary contest, having the biggest house on the block, getting one's name in the paper. We seem to believe that if we receive enough recognition from the outside, we will feel important.

As we grab for the moon and reach for the sky, our spirits are restrained and our hearts grow weary. Jesus witnessed how the people of his day were worn out with all their striving and stress. He invited them to come apart and rest awhile—disciples and crowd. He, the divine physician, would stop the endless fever of acquisition. Jesus offered the gift of peace, the gift of the Holy Spirit.

Lord, we are ill and stand in need of healing. We run here and there, chasing the latest theory and fad. Nothing satisfies because there is a "hole in the bucket," a leak that prevents us from being properly filled. Send your Spirit of peace and wisdom upon us that we might know the grace of humility. Quiet our hearts and minds.

Little Virtues

In seeking our autonomy and independence, we are quick to cast aside the ways and things of childhood. Not only do we separate ourselves from home and parents, we also often shed the virtues and traditions that sustained us in early years. We begin our social climbing seeking to impress others and make our mark. Though we do not see exactly what we want, we know that what we have is too small for our ambition and pride.

Unfortunately, when this happens we throw overboard all those little virtues that nourished our souls and helped to keep us whole: thoughtfulness, courtesy, gratitude with its many "thank you's," humor, tenderness, and kindness. But then, our thoughts turned to distant dreams and notes went off to the "stars and seraphim," human idols and false angels, agents and headhunters. Sad to say, we too often received a reply that kept us returning for more.

Lord, I send you this brief note today. Be patient with our foolishness and waywardness. Send again into our hearts all the little virtues that made us laugh and feel joy. May we climb, not the social ladder, but Jacob's ladder, the one that leads to you.

Returning Home

Can we come home again? Some think not, but the prodigal son proves otherwise. It is possible to arise and go to our God, a God who stands on the hill longing for our return. But we cannot make that journey laden with portfolios, trophy racks, overflowing wardrobes, and ambitions drawing us in different directions. Simplicity calls for an emptying, a downsizing of things unnecessary, so that we move again in the direction of Love-Life-Light.

So, what are the simple things that mediate God's presence? Birds, flowers, bees, laughter, humor… Once again we are invited to see invisible things like elves and leprechauns. Once again the wedding feast has been prepared where a table is set with simple food and drink. To return to community and friendship, to the altar and divine table, to the simple things like love and grace—this is our goal.

God of laughter and tears, God of bumblebees and elves, draw us home once again. We have wandered so far for nothing. We have chased rainbows and pots of gold that were mere illusions. Give us wisdom to see, give us courage to do your will. Come, Spirit of simple things, come.

Prayer Period 10

Community

The spiritual journey is not a solitary track. As social beings we travel together seeking our destiny. One measure of Christian maturity is our capacity to love and be loved, to be deeply involved in the lives of others. The doctrine of the Mystical Body of Christ calls us forth into a graced solidarity; we are responsible for one another, and even for the masses. Jessica Powers proclaims her desire "to be mother of the masses."

THE MASSES

My love had not the openness to hold
so cumbersome a human multitude.
People in bulk would turn the dials of my heart to
Cold.
The mind would bolt its doors and curtly vow
to leave the crowded streets for a while.
And yet if there were patronage in heaven
my passion was to be
mother of the masses, claiming by some small right
of anguish

this piteous and dear humanity.
Out of its need my heart began devising
ways to receive this breathing populace
without the warm oppression of its weight,
and the fastidious mind sought out as good
a multiplicity of motherhood
till the reluctant answer entered late:
I learned from God the ancient primal mother
whose hunger to create has brought forth these,
a multitude in lone nativities,
whose love conceived the numberless, and none
by twos and thousands;
and with Him I bear them
in separate tenderness, one by one.

(90)

Love's Limits

What is our capacity for loving, for embracing the throngs? Many of us are overwhelmed by huge crowds and find it difficult to open the door of our heart. In fact, a certain chill and coldness confronts our hospitality, and we keep ourselves apart from our many sisters and brothers. The mind, too, has its limits and backs off from the crowdedness of life, seeking a less populated solitude. Though minds and hearts have a theoretically huge capacity, when confronted with the practicality of daily life, they run for cover.

Love still has its passions and deep desires even though it struggles to actualize them. In this poem we see someone whose passion is grounded in compassion, in "being-with" this thing called humanity, so piteous and so dear. Here arises the desire to nurture, to mother, as one sees the anguish and beauty of fellow pilgrims. It is a desire for family, for community, for communion. It is grounded in the faith-awareness that we are all linked together by the mystery of God's creative love.

Lord, our love is so small and the world's needs are so great. Send your Spirit of compassion into our hearts and minds so that we might embrace the plight and the glory of our sisters and brothers. Help us to give them life, like a good mother, like a good father. Expand our love and open our hearts.

Human Devising

In being what we are called to be, the challenge is one of reception. How does one welcome the huge populace without being oppressed and weighed down? One option might be to simply throw open the doors of the heart and to let in the entire multitude together. But the idea of "a multiplicity of motherhood" does not bring peace. There must be some other paradigm or model for embracing humanity as a whole. Perhaps the answer could be found, though reluctant and late, in the very divinity of God.

We have so many needs, Lord, and from them arise so many plans. Without your wisdom and guidance we lose our way and make choices that lead us astray. Come to our assistance. Tell us again how we can live in solidarity and compassion with all humankind. Enlighten our minds, enkindle our hearts. Then we will know your will and do it with joy and courage.

God's Lesson

God demonstrates how we can come to embrace humanity. As we ponder the mystery of creation, we see God as our ancient, primal mother. From God, all life and holiness flow. In fact, God's passion and hunger to share existence is the source of the human multitude. God's love is so expansive that it gives itself in superabundant ways. But note carefully: each person's birth is lone and unique. God did not create us in batches, whether in two's or four's or thousands.

Herein is the secret of living and thriving in and for community. By emulating God, we are to bear our sisters and brothers joyfully, and to embrace them one by one. Each is to receive our separate and gentle love. In this way we offer the opportunity for dignity to each person; in this way, we recognize the dignity that each already has. Thus, by living in the present moment and seeing Christ in one another, we embrace the human multitude and fulfill our vocation of being "mother of the masses."

Draw us deeply into the mystery of creation, Lord. Let us see the beauty and particularity of your love. In our nativity you create us unique. May we come to recognize the uniqueness of those around us, and empower us to welcome them into our family. Please give us the grace of community and communion.

Chapter 4

Ten Steps to Reading Poetry in a Holy Way

1. Invoke the Holy Spirit

From a faith perspective, all truth, beauty, and goodness come from God. Poetry carries these qualities in a variety of ways. In order to penetrate and reach their depth, it would be helpful to bring more than our own limited intellectual and affective potential to the process. By invoking the Holy Spirit, the Spirit that enlightens us to see, enkindles us to be on fire with love, empowers us to hear and to do, we have a resource of incredible power. Beginning the reading of poetry by humming the first stanzas of "Veni, Creator Spiritus" could well prove to be an exercise of prayerful attentiveness:

Veni, Creator Spiritus,	Come, Creator Spirit, come down.
Mentes tuorum visita:	Visit the minds of your own,
Imple superna gratia,	fill us with your supernatural grace,
Quae tu creasti pectora.	Hearts which you have created.

2. Aloud in Multiple Readings

One should read poetry aloud, and certainly more than once. Multiple readings are called for in order that the tight packaging of poetry might be unwrapped layer by layer. Speaking poetry is important because its hidden music is meant to be heard. Sight reading a score of Mozart is one thing; hearing the composition is an entirely different experience. And, of course, listening to the composition on a number of occasions, leads to deeper appreciation and to greater enrichment.

3. "Videotape" as You Read

A scripture scholar and friend of mine told of a lesson he learned early in life. A mentor advised him that it would be most advantageous to create an "internal video" of what was being spoken while reading the Word of God. You can actually picture Jesus at the Jordan being baptized by John, watch the prodigal son coming down the lonely road, see the tears in Peter's eyes as he went out into the night to weep bitterly.

You can employ a similar method in reading poetry. You can picture Robert Frost's two roads separating in the wood; feel Hopkins' "ooze of oil crushed"; smell e. e. cummings' "ragged meadows of my soul." Each time we read a poem, we can turn on our video camera and fully engage our imagination and all the senses. And in Technicolor, no less!

Indeed, some individuals are more visual than vocal. They have to "see" what the words refer to. Thus, by practicing the art of "videotaping" poems, these individuals participate in a deeper way with the verse in front of them. When done with full concentration, those poem-videos can remain in the memory for years, indeed, a lifetime.

4. Find a Poetry Companion

Members of book clubs testify that their retention and appreciation of books often doubles and triples when they reflect upon and discuss readings in their group. Reading alone is one thing; discussing with others what you have read can abundantly increase the joy and meaning. Finding a kindred soul, one who has the same taste for particular poems, is a pearl of great price. This practice of a dialogic reading of poetry leads to new revelations and deeper joy.

5. Trust Your Body

The body doesn't lie. When you read a verse that stirs your heart, ties your stomach into knots, makes your feet begin to wiggle, you are in the presence of a power that carries meaning and feeling. John G. Neihardt once reflected: "I *knew* it was a fine poem. It had to be; for I could feel the deep ache of it in the middle of my breast."[1] Poetry is holistic in the sense that it embraces the mind, heart, and body. If there is no visceral reaction to a poem, you might want to set it aside and read it again at a later date. If, however, your body becomes alert and empathetic, you should get out your "keeper file" and gently deposit the newly found treasure.

Reading a Poem

"Trust your body!"

A quick response to my slow question:
"Any suggestions on how to read a poem?"

Does the verse cause a shiver down the spine,
or tie your stomach into knots,
or get the heart beating,
or incite a riot in your genes,
or move the soul to fear and trembling?

Your body doesn't lie,
never having learned that fine art.
Dogs cannot pretend like angels do,
(and, of course, we are in-between the two).

Poems must pass through the senses
on their way to your heart.
Trust your eyes and ears,
trust your taste, smell, breathing,
they will tell you the "how" of poetry reading,
more, the "why" of your delight.

(Robert F. Morneau)

6. Read Actively

Reading actively is far different from reading passively, far different from reading anxiously. In active reading, we attempt to engage all our faculties in the matter at hand. The mind seeks meaning, the senses are alert to images and smells and tastes, the imagination locks into metaphors that help it to make associations and gather up new insights. This active reading does not exclude the contemplative, restful dimension of encountering reality. After making a disciplined effort to understand and feel a piece of poetry, you should sit back and let the poem speak to you in its own good time.

In *Walden,* Henry David Thoreau claimed: "To read well, that is, to read true books in a true spirit, is a noble exercise, and one that will task the reader more than any exercise which the customs of the day esteem."[2] The same is true of poetry. It is a noble exercise and a demanding one. It calls for full, conscious engagement if we are to taste the fullness of poetic fruit.

7. Create Atmosphere: A "Poetry Corner"

Someone once shared with me her process of writing letters: she lit a candle, placed a photograph of the correspondent on the desk, arranged flowers—only then did the writing begin. Creating an atmosphere of quiet and receptivity can be of immense help in approaching and appropriating poetic reading. If there is noise and messiness, if there are constant comings and goings, if your schedule is hurried, there will be slight chance of a significant encounter with the work of a poet. To be interiorly disposed demands some degree of external calmness and order and, yes, even beauty.

Construct for yourself a poetry corner: rocking chair, candle, dictionary near at hand. No other type of reading is to be done in this space or during your special designated poetry time. Environment influences our receptivity to degrees and in ways that we often fail to recognize.

8. Read Poetry at High Energy Times

Each of us has a unique energy pattern. Some people are morning folks, ready to go at 5 A.M. Others find that later evening hours are the most productive and conducive to serious thinking and reading. Since poetry demands a considerable amount of concentration, you might want to budget high energy times as most suited for a serious reading of poetry. Otherwise, much of the attempt to break through the code of poetry might become wasted energy with no penetration or absorption.

Not only is energy important in approaching poetry, also significant is pace. Poetry should not be read rapidly. Words and phrases are to be tasted, repeated, ingested, and digested. Also, reading too many poems at one sitting is counterproductive. A single poem read well and assimilated is better than five poems hurriedly read and, for all practical purposes, discarded.

9. Memorize

Memory is a great gift from God. This capacity to retain an event, the love of a friend, a song or a poem, should not remain dormant. When something is put to memory (and done so purposefully rather than just by rote), an intimacy begins to grow that can be truly transformative. All of us have favorite prayers, early childhood songs, maybe even a poem or two tucked away in some corner or other of our memory bank. What a blessing it is to be able to recall a favorite verse on a sleepless night, or to bring to mind some poem to console us in life's sorrows.

Comparative literature professor George Steiner was correct: "What is committed to memory and susceptible of recall constitutes the ballast of the self."[3] And if there's no ballast, there's no stability. Poems keep us from capsizing in the storms of life. They offer visions and experiences as encouragement: previous pilgrims have felt urged to live meaningful, fruitful, courageous lives.

10. *Keep a Poetry Journal*

One of the most fundamental characteristics of being human is paying attention. A method of attentiveness is note taking, jotting down in words the things we see, names of people we've met, facts that expand our understanding of life. Putting things in writing has the effect of validating our experience and enhancing the possibility of deepening the quality of our lives. We refuse to rush from one experience to another without pausing to process them. To paraphrase the old adage: "Experiences unreflected upon dehumanize."

Poetry, given its intensity and concentration, calls for attentiveness. Having a personal poetic journal on an end-table means that there is a willingness to take the poems that come your way seriously, picking out the words and phrases that stir your heart and enrich your soul. Thus, over the years, a treasury of insights and expressions is accumulated that bring consolation and challenge, meaning and beauty into life.

God of love and language, thank you for the gift of poetry and all the great poets who have enriched our lives with insight, truth, and beauty. Grant us the grace to read well and deeply their works, for through them, we often encounter your presence and your wisdom. Send forth your Spirit, this we pray.

Suggested Poems for Prayer

Blake, William
> The Lamb
> The Tiger
> The Little Black Boy

cummings, e. e.
> no time ago
> i am a little church (no great cathedral)
> i thank You God for most this amazing

Dickinson, Emily
> The soul that hath a guest
> This world is not conclusion
> Some keep the Sabbath going to church

Donne, John
> *Death, be not proud*
> *Batter my heart, three person'd God*
> *At the round earths imagin'd corners, blow*

Gilsdorf, Gordon
> *Lyrics for the Christian*
> *A Saint*
> *Three Mysteries*

Herbert, George
> *Trinity Sunday*
> *Matins*
> *Love III*

Hopkins, Gerard Manley
> *Pied Beauty*
> *God's Grandeur*
> *Spring*

Lewis, C. S.
> *The Day with a White Mark*
> *On Being Human*
> *After Prayers, Lie Cold*

Machado, Antonio
> *Last night, as I was sleeping,*
> *The wind, one brilliant day, called*
> *In the shady parts of the square, moss*

Milosz, Czeslaw
> *Veni Creator*
> *Gift*
> *One More Day*

Oliver, Mary
> *The Summer Day*
> *The Ponds*
> *Some Questions You Might Ask*

Rilke, Rainer Maria
> *This is my labor—over it*
> *October Day*
> *I have faith in all those things…*

Seifert, FSC, Edward
> *God Is Not Nice*
> *Pentecost*
> *On the Ridge*

Notes

Introduction

1. *Poems and Prose of Gerard Manley Hopkins*, selected by W. H. Gardner (Baltimore, MD: Penguin Books Inc., 1953), p. 27.

2. *George Herbert: The Country Parson, The Temple*, edited, with an introduction by John N. Wall, Jr., preface by A. M. Allchin (New York: Paulist Press, 1981), p. 184.

Chapter 1
Why Poetry? Seven "Because's!"

1. John Dykstra Eusden and John H. Westerhoff III, *Sensing Beauty: Aesthetics, the Human Spirit, and the Church* (Cleveland, OH: The Church Press, 1998).

2. Lewis Thomas, *Late Night Thoughts on Listening to Mahler's Ninth Symphony* (New York: Bantam Books, 1980), p. 155.

3. *Poems and Prose of Gerard Manley Hopkins*, p. 27.

4. *Ibid.*, p. 31.

5. John G. Neihardt, *All Is But a Beginning: Youth Remembered, 1881–1901* (Lincoln: University of Nebraska Press, 1972), p. 118.

6. Frederick Buechner, *Telling the Truth: The Gospel as Tragedy, Comedy, and Fairy Tale* (New York: Harper & Row, 1977), p. 21.

7. Avery Dulles, *Models of the Church* (New York: Image Books, 1974), p. 24.

8. Ralph Waldo Emerson, "Nature," *The Selected Writings of Ralph Waldo Emerson* (New York: Random House, Inc., 1940), p. 30.

9. *An Anthology of the Love of God* from the writings of Evelyn Underhill, edited by Lumsden Barkway and Lucy Menzies (London: Mowbray & Co., 1976), p. 50.

10. Quoted in *Denise Levertov Poems 1960–1967* (New York: New Directions Books, 1967), p. 32.

11. Wallace Stegner, *Angle of Repose* (New York: Fawcett Crest, 1971), p. 160.

Chapter 2
Jessica Powers: The Poet

1. Dana Greene, *Evelyn Underhill: Artist of the Innate Life* (Notre Dame: University of Notre Dame Press, 1990), p. 3.

2. Gordon Gilsdorf, *Exploration into God: New and Collected Poems* (Green Bay, WI: Alt Publishing Co., 1992), p. 77.

Chapter 3
Selected Poems—Praying with Jessica Powers

1. Hans Urs von Balthasar, *Prayer*, trans. by A. V. Littledale (New York: Sheed &Ward, 1961), p. 12.

2. Kiernan Kavanaugh, OCD, and Otilio Rodriguez, OCD, translators, *The Collected Works of John of the Cross* (Washington, DC: ICS Publications, 1973), p. 487.

3. C. S. Lewis, *The Great Divorce* (New York: Macmillan Publishing Co., 1946), p. 72.

Chapter 4
Ten Steps to Reading Poetry in a Holy Way

1. John G. Neihardt, *All Is But a Beginning: Youth Remembered, 1881–1901* (Lincoln: University of Nebraska Press, 1972), p. 62.

2. Henry David Thoreau, *Walden or Life in the Woods* (New York: Signet Classic, 1960), p. 72.

3. George Steiner, *Real Presences* (Chicago: The University of Chicago Press, 1989), p. 10.

Selected Bibliography

The Selected Poetry of Jessica Powers. Edited by Regina Siegfried, ASC and Robert F. Morneau. Washington, DC: ICS Publications, 1999.

Books published by Jessica Powers

The Lantern Burns. New York: The Monastine Press, 1939.

The Place of Splendor. New York: Cosmopolitan Science and Art Service, Inc., 1946.

The Little Alphabet. 1955.

Mountain Sparrow. Ten poems by Jessica Powers, published by the Carmel of Reno, 1972.

Journey to Bethlehem. Christmas poems, privately published, 1980.

The House at Rest. Privately published, 1984.

Biography

Dolores R. Leckey, *Winter Music: A Life of Jessica Powers: Poet, Nun, and Woman of the Twentieth Century* (Kansas City: Sheed & Ward, 1992).

Robert F. Morneau is the auxiliary bishop of the Diocese of Green Bay, Wisconsin. He is a popular speaker, retreat leader, and an avid poetry reader. His many books include *The Selected Poetry of Jessica Powers.*

BOOKS & MEDIA

The Daughters of St. Paul operate book and media centers at the following addresses. Visit, call or write the one nearest you today, or find us on the World Wide Web, www.pauline.org

CALIFORNIA
3908 Sepulveda Blvd., Culver City, CA
  90230; 310-397-8676
5945 Balboa Ave., San Diego, CA
  92111; 858-565-9181
46 Geary Street, San Francisco, CA
  94108; 415-781-5180

FLORIDA
145 S.W. 107th Ave., Miami, FL
  33174; 305-559-6715

HAWAII
1143 Bishop Street, Honolulu, HI
  96813; 808-521-2731
Neighbor Islands call: 800-259-8463

ILLINOIS
172 North Michigan Ave., Chicago, IL
  60601; 312-346-4228

LOUISIANA
4403 Veterans Memorial Blvd.,
  Metairie, LA 70006; 504-887-7631

MASSACHUSETTS
Rte. 1, 885 Providence Hwy.,
  Dedham, MA 02026; 781-326-5385

MISSOURI
9804 Watson Rd., St. Louis, MO
  63126; 314-965-3512

NEW JERSEY
561 U.S. Route 1, Wick Plaza,
  Edison, NJ 08817; 732-572-1200

NEW YORK
150 East 52nd Street, New York, NY
  10022; 212-754-1110
78 Fort Place, Staten Island, NY
  10301; 718-447-5071

OHIO
2105 Ontario Street (at Prospect
  Ave.), Cleveland, OH 44115;
  216-621-9427

PENNSYLVANIA
9171-A Roosevelt Blvd., Philadelphia,
  PA 19114; 215-676-9494

SOUTH CAROLINA
243 King Street, Charleston, SC
  29401; 843-577-0175

TENNESSEE
4811 Poplar Ave., Memphis, TN
  38117 901-761-2987

TEXAS
114 Main Plaza, San Antonio, TX
  78205; 210-224-8101

VIRGINIA
1025 King Street, Alexandria, VA
  22314; 703-549-3806

CANADA
3022 Dufferin Street, Toronto, Ontario,
  Canada M6B 3T5; 416-781-9131
1155 Yonge Street, Toronto, Ontario,
  Canada M4T 1W2; 416-934-3440

¡También somos su fuente para libros, videos y música en español!

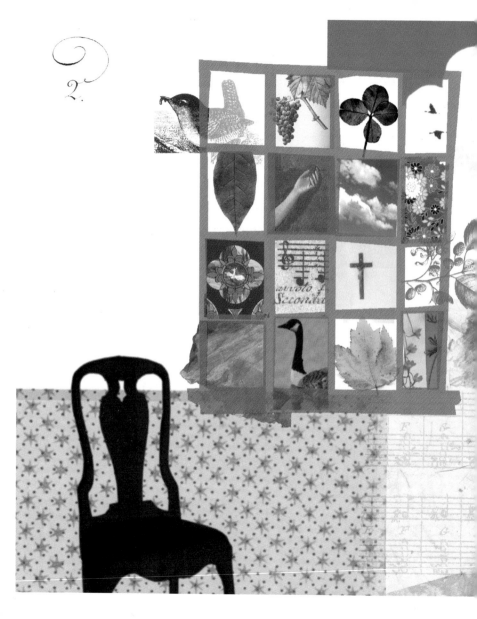